PLAIN
TALK
ON

Peter and Jude

PLAIN
TALK
ON

Peter and Jude

MANFORD GEORGE GUTZKE
PH. D.

ZONDERVAN
PUBLISHING HOUSE
OF THE ZONDERVAN CORPORATION
GRAND RAPIDS, MICHIGAN 49506

PLAIN TALK ON PETER AND JUDE
© 1979 by The Zondervan Corporation

Library of Congress Cataloging in Publication Data

Gutzke, Manford George.
  Plain talk on Peter and Jude.

    1. Bible. N.T. Peter—Commentaries. 2. Bible. N.T. Jude—Commentaries.
I. Title.
BS2795.3.G84   227'.92'077   78-27777
ISBN 0-310-25671-2

Printed in the United States of America

CONTENTS

FIRST PETER
Chapter 1

† † †

PETER WROTE TO BELIEVERS IN CHRIST
(1 Peter 1:1)

Does it mean anything to you that the apostles wrote letters to people who had accepted Christ?

> Peter, an apostle of Jesus Christ, to the strangers scattered throughout Pontus, Galatia, Cappadocia, Asia, and Bithynia (1 Peter 1:1).

These are the opening words of the first epistle of Peter. We want to understand why Peter wrote this epistle. These words are the salutation, which is the heading of a letter. Why did Peter write this letter? What does a preacher preach? Some people believe that after they have accepted Christ they have done all that is necessary. That is like a man who, after he marries and sets up a home, never spends any time at home. Would you think that would be wise? It would be strange if a person accepted the Lord Jesus Christ and understood that he belonged to God, but never worshiped God, and never read the Bible.

Much more follows in the life of a believer after he becomes a member of the body of Christ. Peter is writing to certain believers to tell them this. The salutation is specific. It indicates that the message is for a special purpose. We shall learn that just anybody could not have written this, and, furthermore, it is not written for everybody. He begins, "Peter"—not Simon the son of Jonas, not even Simon Peter—but just Peter. We remember that he started in life called Simon. Jesus of Nazareth said to him, "Men call you Simon but thou shalt be called Peter." Peter is the name given to him after the Lord

7

Jesus Christ had done His work in him. "Peter" is the name of the "saved" man; the man in whom Christ Jesus is achieving His purpose.

Simon, the fisherman of the Lake of Galilee, the man who denied Jesus Christ, is no longer an unlearned and ignorant man. He was beaten by the council; he saw the mighty works of the Lord Jesus Christ. Peter is now writing *as an apostle,* a man sent from God. He was given this message for us; he has authority in this function.

"To the strangers scattered throughout Pontus, Galatia, Cappadocia, Asia, and Bithynia"—not to the whole world. He is not writing this book in the way people write poems for everyone to read. This is a message to certain persons. The word "strangers" refers to the Jewish Christians who were scattered over various areas. The letter is written to believers in Christ. The word "strangers" is used in chapter 2, verse 11: "Dearly beloved, I beseech you as strangers and pilgrims, abstain from fleshly lusts, which war against the soul." "Stranger" is the proper word for a believer in Christ. Any believer in Christ is in the world as a stranger. Peter wrote this letter to believers, whom he looked upon as strangers and pilgrims.

This is pertinent today. The Gospel story is given to the whole world: "Whosoever will may come." The evangelist preaches to everybody. But when a man writes the way Peter is writing, when a pastor speaks to his congregation, or when a man is writing to believers in Christ, he needs to identify them. The epistles were not addressed to the public as such, but were written to people who belong to the Lord Jesus Christ.

THE BELIEVER IS CALLED OF GOD
(1 Peter 1:2)

Do you realize that believers in Christ are called to obey the will of the living God?

> Elect according to the foreknowledge of God the Father, through sanctification of the Spirit, unto obedience and sprinkling of the blood of Jesus Christ (1 Peter 1:2).

These words describe the strangers Peter mentioned in the first verse, those to whom this letter was addressed. It is absolutely necessary, if one wants the blessing of God in Christ, to enter into a personal relationship with Jesus Christ. These are the words we should note: "Elect unto obedience and sprinkling of the blood of Jesus Christ." This is the main thrust of this sentence, and it is the central idea in the New Testament.

Remember, Peter had not been indoctrinated in any school of sophisticated thought. When Peter used the word "elect" he did not refer to books on election. There were no theology books written at that time. He used it as it was in the Greek language: "The called out or recruited ones." He is referring to those who have responded to the call of God in the Gospel. Those who come are the "elect."

This call of God comes not to the favored, or to those who have been given an advantage; it is a call into yielded obedience.

> Take my yoke upon you, and learn of me; for I am meek and lowly in heart: and ye shall find rest unto your souls (Matt. 11:29).

This call is given to all men. It is a call to come to Him, to yield heart and soul, and to obey Him. Blessing comes from obedience to God, to those who willingly respond in obedience to the direction God gives. The believer is called unto obedience in everything.

> Whatsoever thy hand findeth to do, do it with thy might (Eccl. 9:10).
> In every thing give thanks (1 Thess. 5:18).
> Whatsoever ye do, do all to the glory of God (1 Cor. 10:31).
> I can of mine own self do nothing (John 5:30).
> My Father worketh hitherto, and I work (John 5:17).

We have been called into a marvelous experience, a living relationship with God that we might yield ourselves to do the will of God. The word "sprinkling" brings to mind the baptism of Jesus Christ; we speak of being baptized with water and by blood. John the Baptist baptized with water, but he said that Christ would baptize with the Holy Spirit and with fire. Jesus of Nazareth asked those disciples who wanted special favor: "Are ye able to drink of the cup that I shall drink of, and to be baptized with the baptism that I am baptized with?" (Matt.

20:22). They answered they were. No doubt this refers to the baptism of Jesus, the sprinkling of the blood of Jesus Christ. This truth was implied by the apostle Paul, "I am crucified with Christ" (Gal. 2:20). Believers in Christ are the elect, called unto total obedience, and to the crucifixion with Christ, the crucifixion of self.

"According to the foreknowledge of God" means that God knew beforehand all that would happen to the believers; He knew the full course of their living experiences. "He knoweth the way that I take" (Job 23:10). And when difficult things happen, as they may happen tomorrow, the believer will need to deny himself. God will call the believer to that, just as He called the Lord Jesus Christ. The daily round of a believer's life is known to God, and the object of God's will is to promote His purpose.

The life of a believer has been planned by the Father, even as was the life of the Lord Jesus Christ. Each believer has been called to the sprinkling of the blood of the Lord Jesus Christ, that is, to experience crucifixion with Christ according to the foreknowledge of God.

"Through sanctification of the Spirit" implies that the only way a believer can respond at all times to the will of God is to have Christ working in him, the hope of glory. The believer is not left to his memory of the things Jesus Christ has done; he is not left to his own good intentions. The Holy Spirit takes the things of Christ and shows them to the believer. The Spirit activates, makes alive, in the soul, the will of the living Christ all the time. This is what the believer has been called into.

GRACE TOWARD BELIEVERS IS UNLIMITED
(1 Peter 1:2-3)

Do you realize that a believer is always receiving help from God?

Grace unto you, and peace, be multiplied (1 Peter 1:2).

In the first part of this second verse Peter pointed out what believers are called unto. Now he states how it can be done. A

common view about living in faith needs to be corrected.
Mankind, generally speaking, is inclined to admit that in himself is both good and bad. Some persons think there is more
good, and some think there is more bad, and that in becoming a
believer a person tries to be good. People use Jesus Christ as an
example to encourage doing good. This is an error. It was the
error Paul said the Jews made. They tried to be good in order to
do good. They read the law to find out what God wanted, then
tried to do it.

The same is true today. Many people have not been brought
up on the Ten Commandments, but they do know something
about Jesus Christ. When they think about Jesus, they think of
the little Baby born in Bethlehem, and then of the Man who
went about doing good. They may also know that He was
opposed, that He was put on the cross, and that the disciples
thought He was raised from the dead. But with all this in mind,
a person could be wrong in his ideas of what to do. It is not
wrong to remember that Jesus of Nazareth was good and that
He said God expects man to be righteous. The error comes in
the notion that a person can make himself good enough, and
that he can, by trying to be good and doing good, be a Christian.

The truth is that YE MUST BE BORN AGAIN. This will mean dying
to the flesh so that a person might live in the Spirit. In the book
of Romans, Paul points out that believers must die in order to
live. When we read about the sprinkling of the blood of the
Lord Jesus Christ, this means being baptized into His death.
Many sincere people fail to understand that the way to enter
into Christian life and experience is by the denial of self unto
death. It is not in the natural man's heart to yield himself to
death; and that is why we need the great truth that James
pointed out: God "giveth more grace." The grace of the Lord
Jesus Christ is the grace that enables a person to die unto self.
In this way he can accept Calvary for himself.

> For ye know the grace of our Lord Jesus Christ, that, though he was
> rich, yet for your sakes he became poor, that ye through his poverty
> might be rich (2 Cor. 8:9).

That is what Paul said about the grace of God. This was the
grace, the inward strength of Jesus, to die unto self that He

might live forever unto God. Grace from God enables the believer to do His will.

The will of God is to take the human flesh to the cross, and grace gives us the strength to do the will of God. So when Peter writes that "grace be multiplied" he is saying more grace, more grace. James says about our weakness, "He giveth more grace." This is what we need in our homes throughout each day. This grace is available. Peter prayed for these believing people that "grace be multiplied and peace." Peace comes from yielding, and denial of the flesh. The believer should turn to God and yield everything to Him.

> Be careful for nothing; but in every thing by prayer and supplication with thanksgiving let your requests be made known unto God. And the peace of God, which passeth all understanding, shall keep your hearts and minds through Christ Jesus (Phil. 4:6-7).

Peter prays for these believing people, that peace and grace might be multiplied.

> Blessed be the God and Father of our Lord Jesus Christ, which according to his abundant mercy hath begotten us again unto a lively hope by the resurrection of Jesus Christ from the dead (1 Peter 1:3).

Do you wonder how God can be blessed by a believer? The Bible says about blessing that the lesser shall be blessed by the greater. This means that it will be the greater man who will bless the lesser man. How can we bless God? When we say, "Blessed be the name of our Lord and Father, Lord Jesus Christ," we are saying that we want God to be blessed and that man is to bless Him. We think of blessings and benefits as being the same thing; we speak of blessings; and add up all our benefits from God. That brings us to ask, "How can God benefit from us?" What can a human being, even a believer, give to God, since all the silver and gold are His, and all the cattle on a thousand hills belong to God?

Have you thought about your praises? If we do not give God our praise, He will never have it; therefore, praise and thanksgiving are the ways we bless God. The Father likes to see the Son praised; when we thank God for what He has done for us, that is one way of adding to the glory of the Lord Jesus Christ.

Let us look at the words themselves: "Blessed be the God and Father of our Lord Jesus Christ." When we think about "Father," we also think about "the children of God." This brings our attention to being born again. Believers, who have been born again, can call Him Father because He has begotten them again unto this lively hope. The phrase, "which has begotten us again," refers to regeneration, being born again. When we use the phrase "begotten again" we recognize that our first life was from Him. Our spiritual life was also from Him, and that is why we use the word "again." "Unto a lively hope": lively means alive. One could say, "unto a living hope," as a hope "of" living or a hope "in" living. Not only eventually at the last trumpet, when the Lord Jesus Christ will be revealed from heaven and the dead in Christ shall rise first, but now while living in this world, there can be the confident expectation that God will quicken our mortal bodies which were dead in trespasses and sin. He will make us sensitive to Himself through the resurrection of His Son.

Jesus Christ accomplished something in being raised from the dead that, when I believe in Him, is operative in me. When I believe in Him and commit myself to Him, He can quicken me and make me alive, where I was once dead. We have another phrase in this passage, "according to his abundant mercy," which came earlier. But let us think now of the word "mercy." We human beings needed help, and we were utterly unworthy; we had no right to ask for it. But:

> God commendeth his love toward us, in that, while we were yet sinners, Christ died for us (Rom. 5:8).

It was abundant mercy on the part of God that provided Jesus Christ for us.

Whatever our need, God more than fulfills it. We need forgiveness, and He more than provides it. We need strength, and He more than gives it. We need to be reconciled to God, and He more than takes away all the things between us. He provides more than we can ever ask or think, and has done it all in mercy and grace.

INHERITANCE IS RESERVED FOR BELIEVERS
(1 Peter 1:4)

Do you realize that wonderful blessings are already prepared for the believer apart from what he does?

> To an inheritance incorruptible, and undefiled, and that fadeth not away, reserved in heaven for you (1 Peter 1:4).

These words together with those in verse 3 tell part of the blessing a believer receives through Jesus Christ. We should keep in mind that Peter is not introducing the Gospel. He is referring to certain Gospel blessings which the people reading his letter already know about. Perhaps Peter had already preached to them about these matters, and now he is reminding them of what Christ has given to them.

In verse 3 the believer is reminded that he is born again, by the resurrection of Jesus Christ, into a hope for living. Peter adds to this: born again "to an inheritance." If anything comes to me as an inheritance I did not earn it. It is not wages; it is not even the results of my works. I receive an inheritance because someone else gives it to me. A believer receives this inheritance freely because of the death of the Lord Jesus Christ, who bequeathed it to us. Peter calls it "incorruptible and undefiled." This is what Jesus of Nazareth said in the Sermon on the Mount.

> Lay not up for yourselves treasures upon earth, where moth and rust doth corrupt, and where thieves break through and steal: but lay up for yourselves treasures in heaven, where neither moth nor rust doth corrupt, and where thieves do not break through nor steal (Matt. 6:19-20).

Paul wrote:

> For we know that if our earthly house of this tabernacle were dissolved, we have a building of God, a house not made with hands, eternal in the heavens (2 Cor. 5:1).

All believers have in the Gospel the assurance that in Christ they have an inheritance, and this inheritance is in heaven. It is incorruptible, undefiled, and fades not away. Jesus said to His disciples:

> Let not your heart be troubled: ye believe in God, believe also in me. In my Father's house are many mansions: if it were not

so, I would have told you. I go to prepare a place for you. And if I go and prepare a place for you, I will come again, and receive you unto myself; that where I am, there ye may be also (John 14:1-3).

Heaven is not a geographical place. It cannot be located in space. We normally lift our eyes to heaven by looking up because this is a gesture we all understand. But heaven is not localized. And heaven is not something that happens after we leave this world; heaven is now. Jesus Christ taught His disciples to pray, saying, "Our Father, which *art* in heaven." He is in heaven right now. When believers say they have this inheritance reserved in heaven for them, they are not saying that it is something that will take place, which they shall have after they die or when the Lord Jesus Christ comes again. This inheritance, reserved in heaven for them, is something that is set apart in the presence of God for them and is apparently spiritual. It is something that belongs to the very nature of and the presence of God. According to other passages of Scripture, it concerns the redemption of the body. This may be what is referred to in the first chapter of Ephesians when Paul asks that the people might have a knowledge of certain things, including "the inheritance of the saints."

Now what is the meaning of all this? Let us look again at that verse. It may be that this inheritance which believers receive in this way is actually the operation of God in them. It loosens them from their sins and quickens the mortal body to do the will of God. It is incorruptible and undefiled; nothing will spoil it. It is in Christ Jesus. It fadeth not away and is reserved in heaven for all believers. It is something for which Peter felt God should be thanked.

THE BELIEVER IS KEPT BY GOD
(1 Peter 1:5)

Do you realize that a believer receives help so he can keep on believing?

Who are kept by the power of God through faith unto salvation ready to be revealed in the last time (1 Peter 1:5).

This verse is the last of three verses that are one sentence, beginning with verse 3. It is a sentence of praise in which Peter emphasizes three things. In verse 3, Peter emphasizes that believers have been born again unto a living hope; in verse 4, he emphasizes that they are begotten unto an eternal inheritance. In verse 5, he emphasizes that they are kept by the power of God. This profound truth should never be overlooked: God is the Savior. Salvation is the work of God, and is to the glory of God. We should beware of the mistakes the Jews made in trying to produce self-righteousness. This is a natural mistake. Since God is righteous one assumes that believers should be righteous.

One wonderful aspect of God's grace is that it continues forever. The idea that a person is set right by the grace of God and then left to do as well as he can, is not the way it is. The truth is that the believer is set right, and then "kept" right. This is the wonderful blessing in salvation. The person who is afraid he could not "keep up" being a believer misunderstands. It is God who does it; God begins salvation and He will keep it going. The meaning here is "kept unto salvation," which refers to all God does for us by and through Christ Jesus.

This Scripture passage states that salvation is ready to be revealed in the last times. This may not refer to any special period of time, such as a specific era or age in God's plan. Public attention to the phrase, "in the last times," assumes that it refers to some predicted prophecy; as though God has promised certain things to come to pass in some future time. This would imply that a time would come in God's calendar when Christ Jesus would be openly revelaed in His glory to all men. When that hour comes it will be "the last time." If that should be the case, it would mean that the glory of salvation is ready to be revealed when God ends all things. But salvation can refer to the work of Christ, by His indwelling Spirit, in the heart of the believer. This work of Christ may be growth in grace and in knowledge. It has a definite promise of one day completing the work of Christ in the soul.

Salvation begins in the solitary darkness of the soul. It generates faith and obedience to the living God, who will one day exhibit the saved person to the glory of Jesus Christ. Salvation may be something God is working out in the believer. He will one day accomplish it while the believer is still in this world.

We are "kept by the power of God through faith." God will give this blessing to those who honor the Lord Jesus Christ. These are wonderful words of promise, and they are offered in Christ Jesus: those who believe in the Lord Jesus Christ will be kept by the power of God through faith unto a salvation which is ready to be revealed in the last times.

THE BELIEVER CAN ALWAYS HAVE JOY
(1 Peter 1:6)

Can you understand how a believer in Christ could have real joy even while passing through sorrow or distress?

> Wherein ye greatly rejoice, though now for a season, if need be,
> ye are in heaviness through manifold temptations (1 Peter 1:6).

In our last study we noted that God will do wonderful things for believers in Christ Jesus, bringing them out of the natural into the spiritual. Believers are born in this world as human beings, living naturally, as human beings. When they are born again, received in the body of the Lord Jesus Christ by faith, they live a new life which is different from the old life. We call the new life spiritual. The believer can rejoice to know that even in the midst of trouble we have this prospect of salvation.

Peter knew that the people he was writing to were having trouble, and would have more trouble, because believers in Christ do have trouble in this world. He points out that they are able to rejoice even in the day of trouble because of what God has done for them. With regard to this word "rejoice," let me say that when a verb has the prefix "re," it means something is being done again. If you write a letter that needs to be done over, you rewrite it. And when you think about having had joy, you can "rejoy." They had joy when they first realized their salvation, and they had joy every time they thought about it. So they can rejoice to think about it even in the midst of trouble.

This is true of salvation, because in salvation there is a fellowship with God which is unbroken. This fellowship with

God gives the believer joy. He has deliverance from sin. The believer in Christ has freedom, not because he is good, but because God has removed his sin. This is an occasion for joy. He has assurance of effectual power. He will witness by showing others the joys of the Lord, and this will give him assurance. All of this is included in salvation, and when he realizes it, he can rejoice.

All these things: fellowship with God, deliverance from sin, assurance of effectual power, will be given without measure forever, in the grace of God. Peter says, "Wherein ye greatly rejoice, though now for a season, if need be, ye are in heaviness through manifold temptations." The word "heaviness" is a manufactured word in English meaning "heavy-heartedness," which happens while in pain or stress. A person can be downhearted to such a degree that it weights him down; this is possible even while being blessed. "In the world ye shall have tribulation," some of which will be unavoidable, because of human limitations we must accept it. Some will be forced upon us by others, and some will be our own doing. The price we pay for sin is suffering; and when sin is in the lives of others around us, there will be some form of suffering.

Heaviness is the result of a condition. It is not heaviness itself that troubles us, but the sin which causes the suffering. Manifold temptations bother us and the result is heaviness. "Manifold" comes from the words "many fold," and there are many varieties of temptations. There are testings of all kinds. However, this verse is more likely to refer to things that have happened because of wrongs that have been done. It may be that you or a loved one has done something that should not have been done, so you have the prospect of going into court and paying a fine. You cannot be happy about that; but, while you may feel heavy-hearted about this, you can rejoice because all of your family are in good health. Although you do not have reason actually to rejoice in what is happening in this world, you can rejoice in God Himself, in the Person of the Lord Jesus Christ, in the Holy Spirit, and in the truth that is in the Bible.

Peter says, "though now for a season": this kind of heaviness will not last forever. Many different kinds of temptations are hard to bear; some may cause you to feel downhearted and discouraged. But you can remember what God is doing for you. You can remember His plans in Christ Jesus. And having these things in mind, you can rejoice in Him.

TROUBLE MAKES FAITH STRONGER
(1 Peter 1:7)

Can you see that faith shows up most clearly in times of trouble?

> That the trial of your faith, being much more precious than of gold that perisheth, though it be tried with fire, might be found unto praise and honour and glory at the appearing of Jesus Christ (1 Peter 1:7).

There is no better way to learn if a person believes in Christ than to watch him in a time of trouble. Faith is a matter of believing in God, of committing oneself to the living God, and responding to His revealed word. The soul hears some word of God and commits himself to that word: that is faith. Faith is not something that originates in the mind, or committing yourself to a product of your own thought. Faith is coming to know the truth of God which was in Jesus Christ. When God became incarnate in Jesus Christ, the truth of God was lived in actual fact. "He that hath seen me hath seen the Father" (John 14:9).

When we think about the "trial of your faith," we are thinking of the testing of your personal commitment to God who is revealed in Christ Jesus. You acquire your faith by learning the truth of God in Christ Jesus. You live by the attitudes you form on the basis of what you know about God. The testings of these attitudes will occur in the course of manifold temptations.

"The trial of your faith, being much more precious than of gold that perisheth, though it be tried with fire." Peter is saying that when faith is tested in persecution, in trouble, and in stress, it will warrant praise and honor and glory at the appearing of Jesus Christ. For example, when the believer is being tested and tried, what he knows about God in Christ Jesus encourages him to believe that God's hand is in everything and will work for good. We call it Providence that everything is in the hand of God. This comforting fact is what the believer learns in his testings: that as God took care of Jesus of Nazareth, so He will take care of the believer.

Do you have a child in your family who has an illness such as leukemia? Can you still believe that providence is in the hand of God and that He is good? How about a fire destroying your home? These are trials of your faith. The faith the believer has in the Lord Jesus Christ brings him confidence that prayer is the way to blessing. This principle is true, and a believer cherishes it with joy. Since he believes that prayer is the way to blessing, every morning he asks God's care for the day. On a certain morning he may have a collision on the highway. This would be a test to his faith. Would he still be able to believe that prayer is the way to blessing; and that trusting in God is the way to blessing? Consider Job; he trusted God and trouble came to him. This is not to say the believer should not have faith. But the ordinary ongoing of life will confront the believer with situations in which his faith will be tested.

Peter comments that faith is more precious than gold that perishes though it be tried with fire. No doubt you are acquainted with the method of refining minerals. One may find iron, for example, in the clay of the ground. Men take this mineral ore to a furnace and put it in the fire. The hot fire will burn the clay to ashes and harden it into clinkers, while it will melt the metal. Thus there will be a separation of the melted metal that runs out now as pure metal (iron) and the clay which is burned into ashes or in clinkers.

Peter pointed out this is what happens when faith is being refined. There are some aspects of faith that are burned out, but that which is truly dependent upon God will be found to be more precious than gold. Just as furnace fire is used to smelt the impurities out of iron ore, so real troubles cause the believer to rethink his convictions. These may not be as broad as they were originally, but they become what you truly believe. This is what Peter meant when he wrote that even though faith is tried by fire, it may be found unto praise and honor and glory at the appearing of Jesus Christ.

THE BELIEVER HAS JOY UNSPEAKABLE
(1 Peter 1:8)

Do you realize that the heart can have joy so deep and so wonderful that it cannot be expressed in words?

> Whom having not seen, ye love; in whom, though now ye see him not, yet believing, ye rejoice with joy unspeakable and full of glory (1 Peter 1:8).

The experience of a believer rests on or is involved in the person of the Lord Jesus Christ. You as a believer should remember that it is Christ in you that is the hope of glory. To feel that I belong to Christ because I follow His directions is not good enough. To feel that I belong to Christ because I have accepted the Gospel as true is fine as far as it goes, but that is not enough for life and experience. To feel that I belong to the Lord Jesus Christ because I have repented of my sins and confessed my sins, and even have forsaken all known sins, even that is not good enough. That is emptying the pail and cleaning it out; it now has to be filled with something.

Personal communion with the living Lord, looking into the face of Jesus Christ, is the essence of living in faith. The committed believer is a member of the bride of Christ; and the bride has joy in beholding the face of her bridegroom. The nature of a true believing experience can be seen in this Bible verse: "Whom having not seen, ye love; in whom, though now ye see him not, yet believing, ye rejoice with joy unspeakable and full of glory." In spite of not having seen Him, you love Him.

If you did not know about the Lord Jesus Christ you would have no reason to love Him. The Scriptures have told you about Him. We love Him because He first loved us. What does it mean that He first loved us? Does that mean He had sentimental feelings about us? Listen again to the Scriptures:

> Herein is love, not that we loved God, but that he loved us, and sent his Son to be the propitiation for our sins (1 John 4:10).

This is the significance of the love of God. Paul wrote:

> But God commendeth his love toward us, in that, while we were yet sinners, Christ died for us (Rom. 5:8).

So when we have this testimony we can believe Him and we can love Him, "In whom . . . ye rejoice with joy unspeakable and full of glory." This is joy in the Lord.

God's mercy and grace delight the sinner; although I do not deserve it, He comes for me; although I am not worthy, He gives to me. His compassion is balm to the wounded heart. If I have trouble, or if I have anything that causes me to suffer, Christ Jesus can comfort me in kindness and in compassion. This brings joy in the Lord. If I have done wrong or if I have been rebellious, it would be easy to think He would not have anything to do with me. Then I remember that He was "meek and lowly of heart and like a sheep before his shearers is dumb, he opened not his mouth." When he was reviled, he reviled not again. Jesus Christ will help me. I do not deserve it, but He is meek and He is humble; this is a comfort to my heart and fills me with joy.

Then there is His steadfast faithfulness. He will never give up. When I put my trust in Him, He will always be there. This is a wonderful assurance. I have good intentions; I cannot carry them out. He can. This causes me "to rejoice with joy unspeakable and full of glory." We see the glory when something is finished. We see the glory of God in His completed performance. All the benefits which come to me through Christ Jesus fulfill God's purpose and are, in that sense, full of glory. So I joy in these things. My joy is like the joy of one who loves flowers and never tires of looking at them. Some people rejoice in seeing a certain picture, and some rejoice about a job well done. The believer thinks about the Lord Jesus Christ, and he rejoices. Believing is not focused upon the accuracy of the report about Christ, nor the historicity of that report, but on the presence of the living Lord. Though I do not see Him, I believe He is there. He is in me, and believing this fills me with joy unspeakable and full of glory.

THE END OF FAITH
(1 Peter 1:9)

Do you understand that a present faith is required to be saved? That something is going on now in the saved person?

Receiving the end of your faith, even the salavation of your souls
(1 Peter 1:9).

The common understanding of the word "saved" is accepting
Christ. Some will say a certain number of souls were saved,
because that number of people accepted Christ. Many say they
were saved under certain circumstances at a certain time. That
is valid and has its point. Others take the word "saved" in its
final meaning, hoping one day to be in heaven in the presence
of Almighty God, "preserved" in spirit, soul, and body. In their
new resurrection bodies they will say they are "saved," and
that would be true. However, these uses of the term "saved"
do not embody the whole Bible emphasis—perhaps not even
the major Bible emphasis. They certainly are not the whole
truth. The most important aspect of salvation is immediate; it is
going on now. It is continuing. In the present it is incomplete,
and in that sense, imperfect. The Book of Acts says that the
Lord "added to the church daily such as were being saved."

Peter wrote about a certain relationship that believers have
with Christ Jesus. Peter pointed out, as we noticed in our last
study, that the real source of our joy is in the Lord. This joy
originates in what the Lord is presently doing in us. Our faith,
which is a matter of believing right now in Christ Jesus, is not
merely in the accuracy of the report. When we speak of a soul
believing, we do not mean merely that he believes Matthew,
Mark, and Luke told the truth. Nor is that person, when he
says he believes, placing emphasis upon the authenticity of the
promise. God has promised certain things, and we might believe He will do what He promises. This has to do with the
hope of the future. But believing is focusing attention on what
the Lord Jesus Christ is doing "now" in and for us.

Believers can rejoice because they are now receiving the
natural results of believing. They were told that if they believed and committed themselves to the Lord Jesus Christ, He
would work in them and that He would will and do His good
pleasure in them. This actually takes place when a soul believes. In the Gospel, the promise is made that the living Lord
can and will do that now.

Some of the things that will take place in salvation can be

noted. "Receiving the end of your faith" means that this is what has actually been prepared for believers: namely, "the salvation of your soul." Salvation includes healing. When a person receives salvation he is receiving healing in his soul. We read in Psalm 103:3, "Who healeth all thy diseases." This has to do with jealousy, vanity, arrogance, and all kinds of things that concern the individual, especially personal feelings. When you are healed, such sickness of the human ego is taken away.

In the German language the word for salvation means healing. The German noun for salvation is "heil." The relation of that to the English word "heal" is obvious, because it means much the same thing. Salvation is spoken of by Luther as "heilung," which is another word we would translate as "healing." When Luther translated the Lord Jesus Christ's office into English he called Him "Heiland" and that really means "Healer." I am not thinking so much about physical healing by faith, though I would not eliminate that, but I am thinking primarily of the healing of the soul. This is what one receives in the salvation of the soul.

Another function of salvation is deliverance; the prisoner is set free. Salvation provides what the Bible calls "quickening," which is making you alive, sensitive, giving you a new nature. This is part of the blessing in salvation. When you receive the salvation of your soul you are receiving regenerating power which will quicken your mortal body and make you sensitive to do the will of God. Another part of salvation is guidance, something that God does for those who put their trust in Him.

The Gospel gives comfort; God will comfort those who put their trust in Him. And finally, salvation includes communion. A believer can be with the Lord. As Paul said, "The Lord stood by me this night." We can be assured, and truly be given the grace to understand and believe, that the Lord Himself will be with us. It is the receiving of these blessings that fills us with joy and enables us to rejoice in Christ Jesus when we are receiving salvation, the goal of our faith.

PROPHETS FORESAW THE NEW COVENANT
(1 Peter 1:10-11)

Do you know that the work of God in salvation is done in a special way?

> Of which salvation the prophets have inquired and searched diligently, who prophesied of the grace that should come unto you: searching what, or what manner of time the Spirit of Christ which was in them did signify, when it testified beforehand the sufferings of Christ, and the glory that should follow (1 Peter 1:10-11).

A large portion of the Old Testament says that doing the right thing will bring blessing. Something else (something wonderful) in the New Testament is set forth in the work of the Lord Jesus Christ. We learn, as Peter points out, that salvation is something that God does. Abraham looked for a city that has no foundation, whose builder and maker is God. Abraham did not have to build that city. In another place the new Jerusalem, which comes down from heaven, is spoken of. It is already built.

There is something unique about this salvation which is received by believing in Jesus Christ. If it were something that man earned, he could go out and earn it. If it were something man did, he could train and develop his capacities to be able to do it. If it were something man so achieved, it could be evaluated. But that is not the salvation of God in Christ Jesus. This is so different that even the prophets in the Old Testament inquired and searched diligently to learn what this meant (1 Peter 1:10-12). They understood the Old Testament teaching which mainly emphasized law: if man does what is right, he will be blessed; if he does wrong, he will not be blessed: if he does evil, he will be cursed. "Whatsoever a man soweth, that shall he also reap." On the basis of that any man would be lost since man has already done wrong. But the revelation of what God will do in grace and in mercy appears in the New Covenant with Christ Jesus. Living under the Law in the Old Testament was a proven failure; not even good men could do it. "There is none righteous, no not one."

Through the prophets, in Old Testament time, God revealed His plan to redeem man and to save man by His grace. The questioner could bring up the point, "Would it be effectual?" This the prophets studied by diligent research. They learned that this process of salvation by the grace of God would operate through the Messiah, the appointed servant of God, who would come and give His life. His life would manifest suffering unto death, and glories would follow the death that came in the suffering. This is a simple formula and was revealed in Christ Jesus. There would be suffering unto death and afterwards glory.

In the Bible a certain truth was not brought out clearly until the time of the Lord Jesus Christ, namely, the resurrection from the dead. The Old Testament writers knew the Messiah would suffer unto death, and that He would reign unto glory forever. They had difficulty understanding how the same person could suffer unto death and reign in glory forever; because they did not clearly understand nor see the truth of the resurrection. Isaiah spoke of a new sharp threshing instrument having teeth. That was a rather strange expression, but he was intimating that a new instrument would be invented. We understand he was speaking about the Gospel in Christ Jesus. Isaiah also spoke of substitutionary sacrifice.

All the prophets knew that the soul that sinneth, it shall die; but they also knew a sacrifice could be offered in their ritual in place of the sinner, and the sinner could be saved. This was pointing forward to the day when, according to Isaiah 53, the servant of God would die, and "all we like sheep" who have gone astray would be saved through Him. Our sins and our iniquities would be laid upon Him, and by His stripes we would be healed. Jeremiah spoke of a New Covenant when God would write His words in the hearts of men and put His Spirit within them. Ezekiel spoke in the same way of a New Covenant. Daniel spoke of a New Kingdom, the Kingdom of Heaven that would be revealed from heaven, as over against the kingdom of men.

The prophets knew that they had in themselves some intimation of what God would do in Christ Jesus. They knew the Scriptures; they had the actual ritual practices of the tabernacle, all the worship services. Certain events had been carried out in their history which God had overruled and supervised;

and certain things He had shown to individuals. They put all these together and studied, trying to find out what this meant. They had reached the point that the Holy Spirit had testified that this Christ, the Messiah, the One whom God would send, would suffer unto death. They also had learned about the glory that was to follow.

In the 11th verse the little pronoun "it" can be changed to "He," for the Holy Spirit. The prophets had the revelation of the suffering of Christ. They had the revelation of the glory that was to follow, and they searched, trying to find out how those things could be true. Some of the old scholars figured out there must be two Messiahs: one would die as in the 53rd chapter of Isaiah and one would rule, as in the 11th chapter of Isaiah. We shall note in our next study just what was revealed unto them.

PROPHETS WROTE FOR OUR TIME
(1 Peter 1:12)

Did you know that what was preached in the Gospel even the angels in heaven would like to understand?

> Unto whom it was revealed, that not unto themselves, but unto us they did minister the things, which are now reported unto you by them that have preached the gospel unto you with the Holy Ghost sent down from heaven; which things the angels desire to look into (1 Peter 1:12).

The apostle Peter referred to what the prophets tried to find out about the grace of God which would be revealed in the New Covenant, in the Gospel of the Lord Jesus Christ. Peter commented on the salvation which we have as believers in Christ. God will do something in their hearts; something through them and in them and for them in Christ Jesus; this was promised in Old Testament times. The prophets who predicted this New Covenant searched in themselves as to what this could mean.

This salvation in Christ Jesus was not revealed to the ancients. Peter commented that the prophets had predicted it would come, and they had been eager to learn the facts. They had been told this manifestation of the grace of God, that we now know in Christ Jesus, would come later. Inasmuch as the prophets learned that this revelation would come later, it is obvious that what they wrote was not written for themselves but for others.

In this statement by Peter a number of truths are implied. This new salvation would be the work that God does in believers to bless them and to give them joy and peace in Himself. God would work in believers to will and to do of His good pleasure. This new procedure would not be something that would come from man's efforts. This would be a work of grace by the free will of God, without man deserving it. Paul said about this:

> But God commendeth his love toward us, in that, while we were yet sinners, Christ died for us (Rom. 5:8).

This was known to a number of prophets, not just one. Predictions are found in the writings of Jeremiah, Ezekiel, and Isaiah. Some people might say that to understand the prophecies in Isaiah, Amos, Micah, and Hosea we would need to know what had happened then. Peter denies that. The message was not for that ancient time; it was for our learning.

Revelation is the work of the Spirit of Christ. The prophets searched diligently to learn when this would happen which the Spirit of Christ in them predicted. The prophets were not great scholars and philosophers who researched and came up with ideas of their own. This was the work of the Spirit of Christ and what the prophets wrote has now taken place.

The message the prophets spoke about was reported by the preachers of the Gospel in New Testament times. These things were predicted by the Holy Spirit, who came down from heaven. The Holy Spirit did not originate these things as from a human point of view. The Holy Spirit was sent from heaven just as the Lord Jesus Christ came. The Holy Spirit is the third person of the Godhead, sent to help interpret the Gospel and make it real to us. "Which things the angels desire to look into." Angels do not know everything. What happened to Jesus of Nazareth upon earth was astonishing to them and they wanted to understand it better.

SPECIAL GRACE FOR BELIEVERS
(1 Peter 1:13)

Have you any idea what is to be brought to believers through Jesus Christ at His revelation?

> Wherefore gird up the loins of your mind, be sober, and hope to the end for the grace that is to be brought unto you at the revelation of Jesus Christ (1 Peter 1:13).

This verse is the beginning of a new line of thought. Believers in Christ have something to look forward to and they would be wise to get ready for it. In the first twelve verses of his first letter Peter has recalled very important truths to believers. The fact that Christ Jesus could die and be raised from the dead was so amazing the angels wanted to understand it. Perhaps it was true that the angels were particularly interested in the death of Jesus of Nazareth, because this sacrifice was not necessary. The Son of God had been with the Father before the world began. He could say, "Glorify thou me with the glory that I had before the world began." But in His grace Christ laid aside this glory and became in fashion as a man, doing what was necessary for the saving of the children of man. This involved the sufferings of Christ unto death, and the glory of His resurrection.

"Gird up the loins of your mind." We do not use that language ordinarily; it is doubtful any father would tell his son to gird up his loins. He would more likely say, "Roll up your sleeves." In those days men dressed in something like a cloak, a sort of flowing cape, which would get in the way when they were working. They had a practice of tying a rope around it as a sash. Thus they girded themselves so that they could go about their work. We see men roll up their sleeves as they prepare to do something.

When Peter said, "Gird up the loins of your mind," he meant they should be attentive, serious. "Hope to the end for the grace that is to be brought unto you at the revelation of Jesus Christ." Hope is something one does. It is an exercise of the will. It is almost like "believe"; you believe in the Lord, and you hope for the things He has promised. Hope is the confident expectation that what was promised will be realized. One is to hope to the end for the grace that is to be brought unto you. "To the end." I do not think that is merely a terminus but to that end, that purpose, or that objective. The believer should open his heart to God.

"At the revelation of the Lord Jesus Christ." It is possible this means the end of the world, at the time the function of Christ is to be fully realized. The soul believes in and receives Him; and He will be in the believer, lifting him to the will of God. Or, this could be the fulfillment by Jesus Christ when the promises of God have been activated in the believer. Thus certain grace would be given, which would enable the believer to suffer unto death, and to be raised from the dead into newness of life.

This revelation of Jesus Christ is the result that intelligent, diligent faith will bring to pass in the believer. When a soul really believes in the Lord Jesus Christ certain things will follow, and the believer will have grace for living in the will of God.

BELIEVERS SHOULD BE HOLY
(1 Peter 1:14-16)

Do you know what holiness means?

> As obedient children, not fashioning yourselves according to the former lusts in your ignorance: but as he which hath called you is holy, so be ye holy in all manner of conversation; because it is written, Be ye holy; for I am holy (1 Peter 1:14-16).

Here Peter pointed out what believers are called to do. He will present more and more of this truth as we go along. As this epistle unfolds, Peter shows us how believers can collaborate in getting the blessing of God, which depends on what they do. He uses several figures of speech; one of them is here: "As obedient children." Believers have been born again. Peter said believers are to be as obedient children. The Father will lead them in what they are to do, and they are to be obedient unto Him. They are to do as instructed by God, coming when they are called of God, and following as they are led by Him, not fashioning themselves according to former lusts (strong desires). The "natural" person has interests which need to be kept under control, otherwise the believer will develop into the kind of person God does not want him to be.

Before I understood that I was to rule over my flesh rather than trust my flesh, I would have been inclined to do anything I could. I would have been guided by my tastes or my pleasures or preferences without being aware that I was self-centered and egotistical. But now I am no longer ignorant of the reality of things, because I have seen Christ Jesus. I know now what God prefers because the Lord Jesus Christ always did the things which pleased His Father.

"But as he which hath called you is holy, so be ye holy in all manner of conversation." Think of the word "holy" as "wholly," the whole thing, one hundred percent. "Conversation" is a general word that refers to manner of life. "All manner of conversation," then, refers to all manner of life; every conceivable situation, whether in the home, office, among friends, or with strangers. It means being holy in all activities because it is written, "Be ye holy, as I am holy." That is the way it was in the Old Testament; and this has always been the way of God. He is one hundred percent.

This is what Peter was pleading for. These believers might not be strong and they might not be perfect, but they would be sincere, and they would try to do what God would want them to do. So Peter wrote, "As obedient children" (those who are doing what their Father wants them to do) "not fashioning yourselves according to the former lusts in your ignorance" (not developing your character and personality according to the way it used to be when you wanted to live your own way in a kind of mixed-up business). Nothing should be left out of the will of God, or be added to the will of God. The way God wants it is the way we should want it.

BELIEVERS SHOULD REVERENCE GOD
(1 Peter 1:17)

Do you realize that the person who believes in God should walk carefully, in reverence before God?

> And if ye call on the Father, who without respect of persons judgeth according to every man's work, pass the time of your sojourning here in fear (1 Peter 1:17).

If you count yourself a believer in Christ you will call on God; in doing this you must remember He judges according to every man's work. You are calling upon Someone who will play it straight, and if you want to do what is right you will pass the time of your sojourning here in awe of God. The people who believe in God should be most careful of their conduct. It is common to hear about the ungodly acts of ungodly people. We are shocked that these ungodly people act in this way, yet what they are doing is quite natural.

The real scandal with regard to conduct is the ungodly action of godly people, those who claim to know God. For instance, we sometimes hear that nobody reads the Bible any more. Do you? A man who does not have any confidence in the Bible does not read it. Why should he? He does not believe in it. You say, "It is the Word of God." I know that it is the Word of God. You will say, "He will lose." I know he will lose. He has already lost everything, so it is to be expected that he does not read the Bible and he does not pray. But how foolish and how wrong it is for people who believe in God not to read the Bible and not to pray.

Here is a man who says he is in favor of missions, but he never gives anything. Here is a man who favors seeing souls saved but he never invites anyone to church. This is a scandal and it is what Peter talks about. Let us look further at this phrase that refers to God: "Who without respect of persons judgeth according to every man's work." God will be fair in dealing with people. He looks down upon us, and if we are wrong we will be disapproved; if we are right we will be approved. God is Judge of all the earth, and if you pray to Him and trust Him, then you will pass the time of your sojourning here in fear.

"The time of your sojourning" will remind you of the phrase at the beginning of the book: "Peter, an apostle of Jesus Christ, to the strangers scattered throughout . . . ." This referred to the believers who have put their trust in God, and who are like pilgrims here. Since they are like strangers in this world, they spend the time of sojourning (which is temporary) in fear. They are like tourists passing through. While they travel in this way, they should act with responsibility. It is true they are just passing through, but God is not passing away. Their relationship to Him does not pass away. They will be with God forever and ever. Meanwhile, they can pass the sojourning of their time here in reverence and in awe. This is what is meant by "in fear." They will be aware that God knows and sees all things, and they will be very respectful to Him.

God is Almighty God, and is entitled to all the reverence, the respect and propriety toward Him of which they are capable. They can come close to Him. They will be passing the sojourning of their time here in fear in order that they will be blessed.

REDEEMED BY THE BLOOD OF CHRIST
(1 Peter 1:18-19)

Is it clear to you that every human being needs to be redeemed?

> Forasmuch as ye know that ye were not redeemed with corruptible things, as silver and gold, from your vain conversation received by tradition from your fathers; but with the precious blood of Christ, as of a lamb without blemish and without spot (1 Peter 1:18-19).

In these words Peter reminds the believers of their redemption, of the price that was paid for them. This word "redeemed" is a word used with the word "mortgage," an unpaid obligation. Paying off a mortgage is the operation of redemption. The souls of these believers had been under bondage to the kind of life they had received from their fathers.

The word "conversation" does not refer so much to spoken

communication as to the daily life. The Greek word used here means the manner of life. "Vain conversation" is a way of life that is empty. These people were committed to doing things the way their fathers had done. This did not make any contribution to their personal experience. The people tried to do the will of God by keeping rules and regulations. They tried to win the blessing of God through traditional practices, such as observing special days of worship. On the Sabbath day they would come to worship God in a special way; if it was not the Sabbath, the worship should not be the same. On the Sabbath day there were things they should not do. The same was true of various other holy days. Just as it is today, some people would feel there is special significance in going to a church service. This would be a performance God wanted you to go through so you would earn something.

Religion for many is a matter of rules and regulations. There can be all kinds of special ways of doing things: mental patterns; special doctrines; certain ideas about the sacraments, such as taking the Lord's Supper or of baptism; and social patterns. Some persons will worship God in various ways. But when worship is shared only because it is considered the right thing to do, or because others have done this before (letting old customs become the responsibility) the worshiper is going through an empty and vain procedure. The deliverance from all this is through Christ Jesus. How? The believer is redeemed not by paying penalties or fines, but by yielding himself into Christ, into His death and resurrection.

The blood of Christ refers to the death of Christ on Calvary. The truth is not so much that He died for the believer, but that in Him the believer died when he was crucified with Christ. Christ is crucified with the believer, a Lamb without blemish; an innocent, holy substitute offered in behalf of the believer. Now the believer belongs to God through the Lord Jesus Christ. Of course, it follows that when the believer belongs to God he will keep the rules and he will give all that he can. He will attend church, but he will not do these acts in order to get right with God. He will do these things because he is right with God.

THE BELIEVER'S HOPE
(1 Peter 1:20-21)

Do you know that Jesus Christ did something in His death and in His resurrection that opens the way into spiritual living for believers?

> Who verily was foreordained before the foundation of the world, but was manifest in these last times for you, who by him do believe in God, that raised him up from the dead, and gave him glory; that your faith and hope might be in God (1 Peter 1:20-21).

In this portion Peter said some important things about the Lord and about believers. What Peter wrote was short and compact. In order to understand Jesus of Nazareth it is important to remember that He was the Son of God; to think of Him only as a human being will not enable anyone to understand what He did. The Scriptures record, "In the fullness of time, God sent forth His Son." When the Lord Jesus Christ was here upon earth He looked into the face of His Father and prayed, "Glorify thou me with the glory I had with thee before the world began." No one else could say such a thing.

The Lord Jesus Christ had lived before He came into this world; He had been the Son of God. When the angel told Mary she would give birth to a child conceived by the Holy Ghost, the angel said:

> The Holy Ghost shall come upon thee, and the power of the Highest shall overshadow thee: therefore also that holy thing which shall be born of thee shall be called the Son of God (Luke 1:35).

The apostle Paul, in writing about Jesus Christ, said that Jesus did not remain equal with God (Phil. 2:6). Christ emptied Himself, made Himself of no reputation, and took upon Himself the form of a servant. Becoming a man, He humbled Himself unto death, even the death of the cross. In all this we are to feel that the Son of God came into this world as the Babe of Bethlehem to perform a certain function in agreement with His Father: living, dying, and being raised from the dead as Jesus of Nazareth, and then openly shown to be Christ the Lord.

Notice what else Peter says about Him, ". . . who verily was foreordained before the foundation of the world." The word "foreordained" means assigned to this function beforehand. It was the purpose of Almighty God, the Father, that the Son of God should take His flesh to death, and through death into the very presence of God. This particular work was planned by God, and the Lord Jesus was foreordained to serve in this function before the foundation of the world. This was in the mind of God before He made the world.

"Manifest in these last times." Light makes "manifest"; it enables a person to see things. "In these last times" may refer to the final stages of God's plan. He created heaven and earth and put man here, starting the whole process which culminated in the death and resurrection of the Lord Jesus Christ and in His ascension into heaven where He is waiting now for the last act in God's program. Thus, "the last days," the end of God's whole plan, could have begun at the time of Jesus. This phrase might also mean God's plan, in its final stages, for the believer. However, this work of the Lord Jesus Christ must be understood by the believer in order to be operative in the believer. Peter wrote that it was "manifest for you." The believer must understand Christ Jesus dying for him, being raised from the dead, and going into the presence of God for him.

If these things had been done somewhere else on another planet, or even in the very presence of God in heaven, they would not have accomplished their purpose. It had to be done here, for the believer's sake. It was openly shown in these last times for the believer, "who by him do believe in God." Believers believe in God through believing in Jesus Christ. They look for the results of God's grace and mercy which He demonstrated in Jesus. When a person says he believes in God through Christ, he does more than say he believes there is a God. The devils, "in fear and trembling," believe in God. The believer in Christ not only believes about God, but he trusts himself to God in Jesus Christ: that God will do in and through him what God did in Jesus. The believer is looking for results which God promised. God will quicken his mortal body even as He quickened Jesus' body in the resurrection.

That is the route every believer must take: "That your faith and hope might be in God." The faith of the believer is that he will be raised into newness of life. The Christian believes that he will have God's power in his life, just as Christ Jesus did after His resurrection.

BELIEVERS SHOULD SEEK TO HELP OTHERS
(1 Peter 1:22)

Do you realize that zeal is a mark of a real Christian?

Seeing ye have purified your souls in obeying the truth through the Spirit unto unfeigned love of the brethren, see that ye love one another with a pure heart fervently (1 Peter 1:22).

Here Peter gave advice to believers in Christ about developing their spiritual lives. After a person becomes a believer, he should grow; this is possible, important, and even necessary. The one element that brings the soul to the Lord is what the Bible calls truth, a broad term that I am not sure anyone can define to everyone's satisfaction. When I speak of the "truth" I speak of a true situation, the facts of existence as they are.

"Seeing ye have purified your souls in obeying the truth." What would this truth be? It was probably the truth about God and the truth about man. The truth about God can be seen in the universe. God is Creator; He is the Sovereign and the Keeper. He overrules everything and is in control. He is the Judge, the One before whom everyone must stand. God is the Savior for those who have been judged at fault and wrong, but who are contrite. Finally, as we see in the person of Jesus Christ Himself, God is the Father. When a man knows this truth, it can affect him. Just as God is the Creator, man is the creature. Man did not make himself. Man did not even design himself. God in providence watches over all things, and man is dependent. Man cannot create a thing. Man thinks about the fact God is Sovereign and is bewildered about himself.

When a person realizes God is the Judge who sees and evaluates things for what they are, he realizes that man is sinful. When the person thinks of the fact that God is the

Savior, he is reminded that man is doomed. When that person thinks of God as Father, he remembers that those who accept the Lord Jesus Christ as Savior become God's children. This is truth.

I have sketched the truth about God and man. What does this situation say to you? The situation becomes real, significant, and operative when man, the creature (dependent, bewildered, sinful, doomed creature) honors and turns to God, trusting in Him. Man cannot know this truth about God and about himself except by the Holy Spirit of God, who not only gives man a sense of these spiritual realities but also communicates to man the will of the Lord Jesus Christ. The Son of God obeyed His Father; and this is the will that is communicated into the believer's heart by the Holy Spirit.

As the believer obeys the truth which is revealed to him by the Spirit, he purifies his soul. We ask ourselves what it is that makes the soul impure. In what sense does he purify it? It is the ego that impairs it and makes it impure. It is self-centeredness that is evil. The denial of the ego and the repudiation of self come by obeying the will of God. The Lord Jesus Christ said, "I do nothing of myself. I do always the things which please my Father." When the believer, led by the Holy Spirit, obeys the truth, he purifies his soul by denying himself. When he does this, he has denied selfishness in obeying the truth through the Spirit, as He has revealed these things unto him.

"Unto unfeigned love of the brethren." "Unfeigned" means "sincere" love of the brethren. Now pause for a moment. This word "love" is not "sentiment." In the New Testament, "love" does not mean that one has inward emotion. The New Testament teaches that "love" signifies "seeking the welfare of." Believers have denied selves in obeying the truth of God and man through the Spirit unto an unfeigned, genuine love for their fellowman. Peter wrote, "Keep it up," "See that ye love one another with a pure heart fervently." He urged believers to continue this regard for the welfare of others with zeal. The attitude of a believer should not be casual. He will not do anyone harm, but in addition he is supposed to be fervent, actually wanting to help other people, with no concern about self. Pride and vanity are impure. By following these precepts, the believer will carry out what Peter urged upon his people.

THE WORD OF GOD IS FOREVER
(1 Peter 1:23-25)

Do you understand that the spiritual life of a believer comes from the Word of God that never changes?

> Being born again, not of corruptible seed, but of incorruptible, by the word of God, which liveth and abideth for ever. For all flesh is as grass, and all the glory of man as the flower of grass. The grass withereth, and the flower thereof falleth away: but the word of the Lord endureth for ever. And this is the word which by the gospel is preached unto you (1 Peter 1:23-25).

This Scripture points out that the spiritual life of a believer is grounded in the Word of God, which is preached by the Gospel. Obviously, no one is a believer by his own wisdom; no one is that good. Or by his own energy; nobody can do that much. Being a believer in Christ is not a degree of character that is achieved by obeying rules or by accomplishment. In our last study we saw that believers had purified their souls in obeying the truth. That could sound as though the believers had been active in their own efforts, because they had purified themselves. But in these verses, Peter makes it plain that the background of such activities and such purifying was being born again by the Word of God. It was because they were born-again believers that they purified themselves. This "word of God" refers to the promises of God which are to be found in Scripture, the plan of God that is shown forth in the Bible from beginning to end, that man on earth should obey God in heaven. This is the whole idea involved in salvation.

God will not make man climb the highest mountain or run the fastest mile or do the most work in order to be saved. The call of God is direct and simple: anybody can come. The person who comes yields himself and receives the promises of God. These promises of God will be the origin of the believer's spiritual strength. The believer is born again not of corruptible seed. When we think about corruptible seed we may think of the seed of man, which is corruptible. Being born of the seed of man will not only refer to the physical, but it will also refer to the mental, the social, the intellectual, and every other phase of a person. Whether in body or mind, what comes from man is corruptible, and it can go wrong. Believers were born the first time of corruptible seed, but the second time of incorruptible seed, "by the word of God that liveth and abideth forever." The Word never dies, nor is it shaken.

Any child born of human parents has a body that can get sick and die. Anything man produces has a limit to it. He was born of a corruptible nature, but when he is brought into touch with this Jesus of Nazareth and with the Scriptures, he produces from incorruptible seed. The incorruptible man liveth and abideth forever. This is explained in the following Scripture passage:

> For all flesh is as grass, and all the glory of man as the flower of grass. The grass withereth, and the flower thereof falleth away: but the word of the Lord endureth for ever (1 Peter 1:24-25).

What is grass? Grass springs up, dries out, then wastes away. It never lasts. The flesh of man is as grass, and all the glory of man is as ordinary natural flowers. This seems strange to people. All we have in world "art" is what human beings are able to achieve. We speak of "imperishable art" and of "eternal beauty" and so on, but these are just terms. Everything that people make can come to naught. If a person paints a picture, the canvass can be burned; if he carves a statue, it can be broken; and if he builds anything, it can be burned. Everything in art, science, and literature is as the flower. Flowers can be beautiful but they cannot last. This is what Peter points out. But the Word of the Lord endures forever. Whatever one receives from the Lord is eternal.

The Word of the Lord in the Scriptures will speak to the heart. It will speak about the grace of God that is forever and ever. It will speak of the call of God to come to Him. It promises that if anyone comes to Him he will be with Him forever and ever. It will speak about the warning of the judgment of God that is forever and ever. We remember how the psalmist said, "For ever, O Lord, thy word is settled in heaven" (Ps. 119:89). In that word of God is the promise of salvation. "But as many as received him, to them gave he power to become the sons of God, even to them that believe on his name" (John 1:12). Not for a little while, but forever. "Behold, what manner of love that Father hath bestowed upon us, that we should be called the sons of God" (1 John 3:1).

When He did that it was forever. This is the word which, by the Gospel, is preached to all believers.

Many people in our day seek to explain the Word of God. I will tell you what the Word of God is: it is the Gospel that is preached to you, written in the Scriptures and preached to all creation, and presented by the Holy Spirit to believers. It is the actual record of what Jesus Christ has done for believers. If a person understands that Christ Jesus came into this world and died for his sins, was buried, rose again for his justification, and ascended into heaven, that person can put his trust in Christ and believe in Him. It is forever. The Word of the Lord endures forever.

FIRST PETER
Chapter 2

† † †

THE BELIEVER SHOULD AIM TO GROW
(1 Peter 2:1-3)

Did you know a believer in Christ can grow by studying his Bible?

> Wherefore laying aside all malice, and all guile, and hypocrisies, and envies, and all evil speakings, as newborn babes, desire the sincere milk of the word, that ye may grow thereby: if so be ye have tasted that the Lord is gracious (1 Peter 2:1-3).

Having pointed out that the believer in Christ is born again with a new and different nature (because he is born of the incorruptible seed of the Word of God), Peter now exhorted believers to nurture in themselves the spiritual life by feeding on the Word of God. He gave, first of all, a negative comment about what the believer must set aside, and then the positive side of what he is to receive. In a sense, each believer has two natures; he has relationship with two worlds. He was born in this world, physically speaking, in a human way. And he is born again spiritually, as a child of God. His first nature is based in his flesh, and the second in his spirit, and his spiritual relationship with God.

We read here some of the attributes of the old nature. "Wherefore laying aside all malice" (feelings that you have towards someone else; perhaps some feeling of jealousy about something; a feeling that in some way another person threatens you), ". . . all guile" (in dealing with other people you are tempted not to be honest; maybe you have a purpose of your own and you are trying to get by with something, a temptation which is purely natural; it has to do with self and comes from the flesh), ". . . all hypocrisies" (two-facedness; we talk to one person, then to another, and have different attitudes; this belongs to human nature but it does not belong to the Lord; you and I are to put off this old man), ". . . and all evil speakings" (this covers a wide range; speaking evil of people; commenting on things about them which may hurt).

Peter urged believers to be "laying aside" all these things which are related to self in relationship to others. This reminds us of Cain, how he thought about Abel with the jealousy, envy, and malice he felt. All such natural evil traits can be laid aside in self-denial, or the more obvious Biblical word, in self-crucifixion. Doing this, as newborn babes starting out, believers should desire the sincere milk of the Word.

In the book of Hebrews a passage deals with this very matter.

> Therefore leaving the principles of the doctrine of Christ, let us go on unto perfection; not laying again the foundation of repentance from dead works, and of faith toward God, of the doctrine of baptisms, and of laying on of hands, and of resurrection of the dead, and of eternal judgment (Heb. 6:1-2).

One might think that the "milk of the word" (the doctrine that would be given to children or beginners) would be mild, like urging new believers about being better and doing good. But here is the truth that should be set forth to beginners. They are to put their faith in God and not man. Baptisms would include the baptism of the Holy Spirit and the baptism of repentance. Believers need to understand these truths. A new believer needs to understand the "resurrection of the dead." He should not wait until the conclusion of a long life to learn this truth. When believers turn to the Lord Jesus Christ and put their trust in Him, one of the first things they learn is that they will be raised from the dead and that they will go to be with the Lord.

If one person should teach another the Gospel of Christ, he should talk about things like this: repentance from dead works; faith toward God; baptism of the Holy Spirit; laying on of hands with the sense of responsibility for work and for witness; the resurrection of the dead and eternal judgment. These are the "milk of the word." Becoming a believer is not a matter of coming part way, starting out little by little. Christ Jesus died on Calvary's cross not a little at a time but altogether. He died for our sins, not for just a few, but for all of them. This is the truth, and these ultimates are to be brought in at the very beginning of our life with Christ. Believers should "desire the sincere milk of the word" that they may grow thereby.

"If so be ye have tasted that the Lord is gracious" (1 Peter 2:3) means that if you have had any spiritual experience you should seek the spiritual truths which have been stated above. If you have any confidence in the kindness of the Lord at all, because the Gospel has been presented as meaning that God forgives you, you ought to avoid seeking any personal, carnal benefits. You should not enter into the things of the Lord with any aim to profit; you should receive the things of the Lord with joy and with gladness, because you have counted on trusting in Him and have tasted that the Lord is gracious. The believer in Christ then, laying aside all malice, guile, hypocrisy, envy, and all evil speaking (putting all that out of himself altogether, as a newborn babe), should "desire the sincere milk of the word," that he may grow thereby if so be that he has tasted that the Lord is gracious. As a believer, you should give yourself over to Him and put your trust in Him, and begin to desire the sincere milk of the Word, by studying the Bible. This would be honest. The believer should take it exactly as it reads and get to understand the Bible so that it may grow in his heart, because that is what God will bless and that is what He will endorse.

THE FUNCTION OF BELIEVERS
(1 Peter 2:4-5)

Have you ever thought of believers being built together as a group for the service of the Lord?

> To whom coming, as unto a living stone, disallowed indeed of men, but chosen of God, and precious, ye also, as lively stones, are built up a spiritual house, a holy priesthood, to offer up spiritual sacrifices, acceptable to God by Jesus Christ (1 Peter 2:4-5).

In a previous study Peter spoke to these believers as obedient children. He called upon them to be holy, even as God was holy; one hundred percent committed to Him. In our last study they were urged as little children to desire the sincere milk of the word that they might feed upon God's Word as a baby feeds upon milk, and grow thereby. Now, in First Peter 2:5 they are spoken of as "lively stones." That expression is unusual; we need to keep in mind that it means "living." These living stones are built together with each other in a fellowship: a group to serve the Lord.

We should note what is said about the Lord:

> To whom coming, as unto a living stone, disallowed indeed of men, but chosen of God, and precious (1 Peter 2:4).

In the Bible, and especially in the New Testament, whenever a stone is spoken of, the reader should remember what is said of a rock. You will recall that the classic use of a rock in the New Testament is as a foundation, "Upon this rock I will build my church." The apostle Paul later said, "For other foundation can no man lay than that is laid, which is Jesus Christ." So when the word "stone" or "cornerstone" is used we should think in terms of a building resting upon one important large rock or stone that will hold it firmly and safely. This is the stone on which the believer rests himself. Because Christ Jesus is the very Lord of life itself, and because all that He does is done in action and movement, the word "living" is used. He is a stone in the sense that He is the foundation, something to rest upon; but He is a "living stone." So we read here, ". . . coming as unto a living stone."

This brings to mind something that has been mentioned both in the Old and the New Testaments: the building of the temple, the House of God, with a chief cornerstone. According to tradition, and the Scripture seems to imply it at the time of the building of the temple a search was made for an adequate cornerstone, when all the time the stone was right there, available. It had been overlooked, and this seems to be the analogy here. Christ Jesus, the foundation upon which they could build, had been disallowed of men. Even today, many people ignore Him. He is not accepted in His claim as the Son of God. Many times He is spoken of as Teacher more than as

Savior. He is often spoken of as a Prophet, not as the Son of God. Many people will offer Him a high title, but not the true one.

When Jesus of Nazareth asked the disciples, "Whom say ye that I am?" Peter replied, "Thou art the Christ, the Son of the living God." Men, generally speaking, do not give to Jesus, the Christ, His place as the only begotten Son of God. "Chosen of God" is what, in the Old Testament, was called "Messiah," and in the New Testament is called "Christ." "Anointed to the task" and precious, means that the Lord Jesus was highly esteemed and was above all others.

When we speak of believers as stones we are to think of them as if they were being used to build a house. Each one would have his place, so when we speak about the believer as being a stone or a brick we are saying each has his place in the wall. This would mean that we are given our places and we are to stay there. We are to be found faithful in whatever is given us to do. Peter wrote of the believers as living stones, being built up as a spiritual house. This did not necessarily refer to a building with roof, windows, and doors. This could be a "house" in the sense of the "house of Saul," the "house of David," or the "house of the children of God": namely, a family, a holy priesthood. The word "holy" means one hundred percent dedicated. Believers are a group of servants who are so dedicated "to offer up spiritual sacrifices" (sacrifices that are of the spirit, not sacrifices of the flesh).

Sacrifices of the spirit are described elsewhere:

> By him therefore let us offer the sacrifice of praise to God continually, that is, the fruit of our lips giving thanks to his name (Heb. 13:15).

Spiritual sacrifices are praise and thanksgiving acceptable to God by Jesus Christ. The praise and thanksgiving of believers would be acceptable to God because they honor Jesus Christ. This is what the believers are called together to give. Peter has been pointing out how believers are called together and built together as a group for the purpose of serving God, offering up to Him praise and thanksgiving in the name of the Lord Jesus Christ.

THE CENTRALITY OF CHRIST
(1 Peter 2:6-8)

Do you realize that Jesus Christ in Himself makes all the difference for the believer?

> Wherefore also it is contained in the scripture, Behold, I lay in Zion a chief corner stone, elect, precious: and he that believeth on him shall not be confounded. Unto you therefore which believe he is precious: but unto them which be disobedient, the stone which the builders disallowed, the same is made the head of the corner, and a stone of stumbling, and a rock of offense, even to them which stumble at the word, being disobedient: whereunto also they were appointed (1 Peter 2:6-8).

Here Peter sets forth how a man's eternal status depends on Jesus Christ. When Almighty God sent His Son into the world to seek and to save the lost, He was offering His beloved Son to man as a basis for man to come to Him. Christ was the Cornerstone upon which any man could build himself before God. Jesus of Nazareth, when He came and lived a perfect life in this world, fulfilled all righteousness and was beyond reproach in every way. But the significance of Jesus did not depend upon what men thought of Him, nor how well they spoke of Him. Rather, His significance depended upon the Scriptures, which said what the term "Son of God" actually meant. In this passage we have a quotation from the Old Testament about Jesus, about the Christ being the chief Cornerstone, which made all the difference for believers.

"Wherefore also it is contained in the scripture, Behold, I lay in Zion a chief corner stone." This is actually the Scriptures reporting something that was said through Old Testament prophets by the Son of God. When He said He was lying in Zion, He means that it was as if He was lying on the ground, in a stone pile. "In Zion" means that He was among God's people. He was exceptional, but He was found among God's people, just like one of them.

"Elect, precious": "elect" means chosen to serve in a special way. Christ Jesus was elect in the sense that He was called or chosen to serve in a very special way. The word "precious" refers to the fact that He was precious in God's sight, as the

Scripture records. "This is my beloved Son, in whom I am well pleased."

A further statement follows: "and he that believeth on him shall not be confounded." This was to be true about the Messiah. Anybody who would believe in Him and trust in Him would not be confounded. When a person is confounded, the state that follows is "confusion." This means to say that he who would believe on Christ Jesus would not be confused, embarrassed, or ashamed. In other words, this Cornerstone—this Messiah—was worthy of all confidence.

"Unto you therefore which believe he is precious." Believers who put Him to the test, who actually trust in Him now, have great reason to have affection for Him. He is able to stand up to every test in which the believer is involved. "But unto them which be disobedient, the stone which the builders disallowed, the same is made the head of the corner." This refers to persons who do not follow the guidance of God's Word and put their trust in Christ, but who stand in the presence of God in their own strength. Such may develop ideas that are not grounded in Christ, but will find that the Lord Himself became the issue. In other words, the stone which the builders disallowed, the same is made the head of the corner. If the builders did not use this big stone, when the time comes for evaluating their building, that stone would be pointed out and they would be asked why they did not use it. Thus Christ would become for them "a stone of stumbling, and a rock of offense, even to them which stumble at the word, being disobedient: whereunto also they were appointed."

The truth is that if I do not turn to the Lord Jesus Christ for help, I have God to deal with in my own strength. Why did I not put my trust in Him? No one comes to God but by Him: "I am the way, the truth and the life; no man cometh to the Father but by me." Anybody coming out of this world into the future world must meet Jesus Christ first. Those who talk as if the Lord Jesus were simply a man who set an example, and treat Him like one of the prophets, will be very much surprised when they reach heaven and find they have to face Him. The believer who comes to the Lord has great wisdom and puts his trust in Him now. When Christ was made the Head of the Corner, He became a Stone of stumbling and a Rock of offense to those who failed to come to Him. These are the people who stumble at the Word, who do not follow through in the guidance of God.

Peter seems to imply that, in the day of judgment, people will stand face to face with God. One of the questions they must face is what they did with Jesus, who was called the Christ. Doubtless there are many phases of the truth that we may know only in part, but relationship to the Lord Jesus Christ is essential.

BELIEVERS HAVE A SPECIAL TASK
(1 Peter 2:9-10)

Do you feel that you know the one thing all believers must tell the world?

> But ye are a chosen generation, a royal priesthood, a holy nation, a peculiar people; that he should show forth the praises of him who hath called you out of darkness into his marvelous light: which in time past were not a people, but are now the people of God: which had not obtained mercy, but now have obtained mercy (1 Peter 2:9-10).

In these words Peter speaks to believers in order to strengthen them in their relationship with the Lord and to stimulate them in their service. These verses focus attention on the believers. There are four things said of them in as many successive phrases: they are called "a chosen generation," "a royal priesthood," "a holy nation," and "a peculiar people." Here are four different categories: generation, priesthood, nation, and people. Now let us look at these four qualifying words: a "chosen" generation, a "royal" priesthood, a "holy" nation, a "peculiar" people. When He calls His people a chosen generation He does not mean they were selected instead of others. That is true, but it is not the point of emphasis here. All are called but some do not come. Those who come are called for a purpose: to serve the Lord.

Let us look at "a royal priesthood." The Bible speaks of

several different categories of servants. It speaks of prophets, priests, and kings. A prophet is one whose function is to tell people the Word of God; he prophesies the Word of God. A priest is one whose function is to lead people in the worship of God; he draws nigh unto God and makes intercession for the people. A king is one who orders, directs, and coordinates the activities of people, and who brings order into their lives. Leadership among the people of God develops along all three lines. Just now Peter is saying that each believer is a priest, the idea being that believers are a royal priesthood, each priest being in himself a king.

We are told in Revelation 1:6 the Lord Jesus Christ has made us to be "kings and priests" unto God. Some people translate that to say "a kingdom of priests." If you say they are a kingdom of priests you are coming very close to a royal priesthood. The word "royal" means that which belongs to the king, and "priesthood" refers to the fact they served God. Thus believers are those who serve God as priests, worshiping and bringing people to the service of God. They also live among other people as kings: they are in control. So believers are spoken of as "a royal priesthood."

The next phrase used is "a holy nation." The word "nation" is a common word meaning all the people in a group, but the word "holy" is the significant word. "Holy" here, as well as elsewhere in the New Testament, can be understood when we think of the English word "whole." By accommodation we have dropped some of the letters and instead of writing "wholly" we now have simply "holy," in the sense of being one hundred percent. "A holy nation" is a nation with one hundred percent of the citizens dedicated to God, totally yielded. Peter said this about believers in Christ.

The last phrase is "a peculiar people." This is most important of all the words we have talked about because the word "peculiar" does not mean funny, nor exceptional in appearance. It means "peculiar" in the sense that it is peculiar to God. I have, for instance, a hat that is my own. That hat is different from any other hat; it is a peculiar hat, it is my hat. The same applies to my clothes, my shoes. My car is peculiar to me; my house is peculiar to me; and my family is peculiar to me. When we speak of a peculiar people we mean a people who belong to

God. The function that will be performed by these people will be one hundred percent.

All of these people, the whole group of believers, had one common experience: they had been called out of darkness into His marvelous light. What this means, among other things about the people of God, who "in time past were not a people, but are now the people of God," is to say that they had not always belonged to God, but now they do. What a glorious experience this is in a Christian. If you who read these words are not sure you belong to God through faith in Christ, let me say to you earnestly and faithfully: you could. "Which had not obtained mercy, but now have obtained mercy." This expresses the truth. These people had lived for awhile in the world outside the mercy of God. They had not sought His face, but now they did. They found the mercy of God and they were now in the company of people God was helping. All of these things were said about these believers in Christ. Thus Peter encouraged them to feel that they really did belong to God in Christ Jesus, and could serve Him.

BELIEVERS ARE STRANGERS IN THIS WORLD
(1 Peter 2:11)

Do you realize that when any believer in Christ understands himself, he knows that he is only a tourist in this world?

> Dearly beloved, I beseech you as strangers and pilgrims, abstain from fleshly lusts, which war against the soul (1 Peter 2:11).

Being a believer in Christ means that a man must see himself as being different from other people. It is natural to want to go along with the crowd. It is easy for us to want to do what others do. Much in life happens to us without our consent or choosing, but much in the believer's experience depends upon his conscious, intelligent choice.

Peter set forth four figures of speech intended to help believers understand themselves. In chapter 1, verse 14 he wrote of believers as being "obedient children" and urged them, "Be ye holy in all manner of conversation." The next figure of speech Peter used was in chapter 2, verse 2, "As newborn babes." This refers to their personal growth. For these people Peter gave this word, "Desire the sincere milk of the word, that ye may grow thereby." In chapter 2, verse 5, believers are spoken of as "lively stones." This was in relation to other believers: each believer will have a certain place that is given to him in the wall and this will be what he is called to do. A believer must realize he is one of the group, and all believers together are to honor God in obedience. In chapter 2, verse 11, the figure used is "strangers." Peter urged them, "As strangers and pilgrims, abstain from fleshly lusts, which war against the soul." The apostle wrote soberly and directly to these people.

He began by using an expression of his affection: "Dearly beloved." He challenged them to self-denial. "I beseech you." No one believer will ever be in a position to command any other believer to regulate the conduct of a third believer. But believers can be concerned that fellow believers should act in the will of God. The word "beseech" implies an earnest request, not a command. "As strangers and pilgrims" really means as foreigners; like an American in Russia or a Canadian in Brazil. We must remember that Paul said, "Our citizenship is in heaven." We do not belong here; we have other goals. We seek peace, rest, and joy; we desire to be well-pleasing to God.

We are strangers in this world, not greatly impressed by what is going on here. We are not greatly depressed if we do not possess much, because we are strangers, pilgrims; we are here only temporarily. "Fleshly lusts" does not necessarily mean something vulgar or immoral. The word "lust" properly understood means strong desire, and fleshly lusts would be the strong desires of a human being. These desires will vary with different people. For instance, with some people this fleshly lust may be making money; with others, gaining social recognition, or gaining fame or fortune. Some are interested in sports to excess, others in amusement or pleasure. Peter says abstain; leave it alone. These human interests war against the soul.

Jesus of Nazareth said, "If any man will come after me, let him deny himself." A believer will not be overly concerned about human matters.

AN HONEST MANNER OF LIFE IS IMPORTANT
(1 Peter 2:12)

Do you understand that in a believer's testimony, actions speak louder than words?

> Having your conversation honest among the Gentiles: that, whereas they speak against you as evildoers, they may by your good works, which they shall behold, glorify God in the day of visitation (1 Peter 2:12).

It is most important for an honest man to act like one. The things of the Spirit are invisible so we cannot look into a man's heart. We can only watch him, and that is why the believer in Christ must be an open witness. "Having your conversation honest among the Gentiles" refers to the manner of life; but part of the manner of life is speech, and speech is heard. Actions are seen but speech is heard. Even an action when it is seen needs to be interpreted. That is why the most significant action probably is a person's speech. What, then, shall we think about the daily speech of a believer in Christ who never refers to the Lord?

At a certain stage in my spiritual experience as a believer, I was not satisfied with my faith nor happy with my personal conduct. It did not seem that things were quite as they should be. I came into fellowship with some people among whom was a woman who was a sincere believer. In the course of our conversation she made this comment, "Don't you know that every time you name His name you will be stronger?" That was many years ago and I find it is true to this day. There are some who judge, when they hear a person talking about the Lord, that that person is putting on an act, trying to appear pious. It is a sad fact that often among believers little is said about the Lord.

If unbelievers never hear one word from me about my faith, am I really honest? Of course, speech is not all. There is the matter of handling money; there is the matter of the Sabbath day; and there is the matter of reading the Bible and praying. In his daily life a sincere believer will worship God, and if he has money, he will give. Reading the Bible is an honest testimony.

"Having your conversation honest among the Gentiles: that,

whereas they speak against you as evildoers." In any community some will criticize believers as being poor citizens, parents, or neighbors. Oftentimes believers are not elected to represent the community because they are outspoken for the Lord. That may be one reason they do not talk about their convictions. Even in the church some are overlooked at times when selection is made of leaders. But "they may by your good works, which they shall behold, glorify God in the day of visitation." When the time comes for judgment the truth about each believer can be recognized. All of this is a way of saying that in the showdown it is actual performance that counts.

THE TESTIMONY OF A BELIEVER IN CHRIST
(1 Peter 2:13-16)

Do you have any idea how a believer in Christ can show his faith?

> Submit yourselves to every ordinance of man for the Lord's sake: whether it be to the king, as supreme; or unto governors, as unto them that are sent by him for the punishment of evildoers, and for the praise of them that do well. For so is the will of God, that with well doing ye may put to silence the ignorance of foolish men: as free, and not using your liberty for a cloak of maliciousness, but as the servants of God (1 Peter 2:13-16).

One may ask how a believer in Christ shows his or her faith. What does a believer "want" to show? If a person is a believer in Christ some things will be true in his life. Deep down in his heart he believes that God is real; that He is the Creator of the heavens and the earth; and He is the Keeper of His creatures. The believer finds that he does not always have full control, and so he begins to think that God is Sovereign. He becomes aware of the fact that God is his Judge; and then, because he has come to know something of God's love and mercy, he knows that God is his Savior. The believer in Christ also knows that man is finite and dependent. Man is sinful, lost. The believer no longer has confidence in himself or in any other human being; he trusts in God rather than in man. The believer in Christ is a child of God, who will care for and protect him. Also, as we have noted, he knows he is a stranger and a pilgrim. The believer is able to live in his situation with considerable quietness and peace, because it really does not matter to him what happens in the world around him. His relationship is with God.

For such a person it is written here, "Submit yourselves to every ordinance of man for the Lord's sake." This means that the believer should yield, whatever the law may be; not only to the good laws but to every ordinance of man, for the Lord's sake. And for the sake of the Lord he will become known as a person who is faithful in his assignments and yielded to the situation as it is, "whether it be to the king, as supreme; or unto governors, as unto them that are sent by him for the punishment of evildoers, and for the praise of them that do well." The believer in Christ may have to deal with governors, so he yields to them, "that with well doing ye may put to silence the ignorance of foolish men."

Whenever the Bible uses the word "foolish" we can remember that "the fool hath said in his heart there is no God." So, with well doing the believer may put to silence the ignorance of foolish men. "As free, and not using your liberty for a cloak of maliciousness, but as the servants of God." A believer is free: nobody has control over him. He is free as far as money is concerned; he does not have to have it. If he has money, he does not have to spend it. If he spends it, he does not have to worry about being without, because money is just something to handle. He realizes its importance but he will not let money dominate him. The Scripture tells him, "Teach us to number our days that we may apply our hearts unto wisdom." The believer in Christ is free, but he does not use this liberty as a cloak of maliciousness. This freedom from the law is not license; he is free from the law but not free from God. He is always under the law of God; he uses his freedom as the servant of God.

Thus the believer in Christ shows his faith by living a humble, submissive life in quietness and in peace.

THE PUBLIC CONDUCT OF A BELIEVER
(1 Peter 2:17)

Do you think if a man sets himself to be a servant of God he will then pay attention to man?

> Honour all men. Love the brotherhood. Fear God. Honour the king (1 Peter 2:17).

This is a very short, simple passage with four direct commands or imperatives. These words were written to believers in Christ by way of helping them to serve in their faith.

It is a common idea that if a man lets his mind and heart be filled with the Holy Spirit he will become so spiritual he will lose all interest in human affairs; but this is not true. It is surprising how people who have never tried to live by faith in Christ will feel competent to talk about living in Christ. This could be true with the natural man, and it could be true with pagans. There are other religions that are natural religions: human ideas about how to get right with God. In certain countries it is popular to be a religious ascetic, and thus to be the kind of person who does not do anything that is satisfying to the flesh. It can follow that such persons become so absorbed with their religious practices they lose all interest in the community. But that is not the Gospel. And that is not the way it worked with Jesus of Nazareth. When a man turns to Christ Jesus, receiving Christ Jesus as the Lord and Savior in his own soul, he will be given the mind of Christ. That seems reasonable, doesn't it? And if a person has the mind of Christ it will not be a frame of his own mind, nor will it be Christ's acting in a certain way. If a person has this mind of Christ he will have operative in him none other than Christ Jesus Himself. If the mind of Christ is in me, I will find myself looking on other men as God's creatures who could be saved, and I will have an interest in them. God is not willing that any should perish, but that all should have everlasting life. Some will perish but it is not what God wants. God's attitude of grace toward all men moves the believer to act kindly toward all men. And because this is so, the believer in Christ is very sensitive in his personal conduct toward others.

Let us look at these four short imperatives. First, "Honor all men" means do not despise anyone. The believer in Christ does not condemn or rebuff anyone. There are people who are not good, but the Lord Jesus Christ looks upon them with compassion. If I have the mind of Christ in me, I also can look upon them with compassion. There will be no gossip; I will not say anything about anybody to his hurt. There will be no exploiting the poor or taking advantage of the weak. The foolish and the uneducated I will treat with respect.

"Love the brotherhood." This refers to fellow believers. The believer in Christ will give loving attention to them because a special communion exists among believers. This brotherhood is not in the flesh; it is not between human beings. This is not the poet's dream of the brotherhood of man; this is a special affection that believers have toward other believers because Christ is in them, and they are truly brothers.

The next statement is, "Fear God." This is not slavish fear or abject terror, but the wholesome reverence of a believing man toward his heavenly Father. In the Bible this kind of fear toward God is spoken of as keeping His commandments. An attitude of reverence toward God is what fearing God means. "Honor the king" refers to the government, the leader. The believer in Christ will show respect and consideration to those who are over him in authority, not because of the personal worth of that individual, but because of his office.

What I have set before you refers to the public conduct of the servants of God. If a man lives as a servant of God, he will have an attitude of grace toward all men. It will show up like this: he will treat all men honorably; he will love other believers; he will reverence God; and he will respect those in authority.

A BELIEVER IN CHRIST IS HUMBLE
(1 Peter 2:18-20)

Do you realize that a true believer in Christ will be humbly patient even when he is being unfairly treated?

> Servants, be subject to your masters with all fear; not only to the good and gentle, but also to the froward. For this is thank-

worthy, if a man for conscience toward God endure grief, suffering wrongfully. For what glory is it, if, when ye be buffeted for
your faults, ye shall take it patiently? but if, when ye do well, and
suffer for it, ye take it patiently, this is acceptable with God
(1 Peter 2:18-20).

Remember, this admonition is not for the people of the
world; this is for believers in Christ and it guides them into the
will of God and into His blessing. This is astonishing guidance.
That word "froward" is an old English word which means the
hard-boiled or tough-minded ones. It is thanksworthy if a
man, for conscience toward God, endures grief, suffering
wrongfully. This sets before a believer the idea that it is
thanksworthy before God if he accepts the suffering that comes
to him as unto the Lord, even though he is wrongfully treated.

In verse 20 Peter argued we should not take credit if, when
buffeted for our faults, we take it patiently, "but if, when ye do
well, and suffer for it, ye take it patiently, this is acceptable
with God." In the Book of Acts we are told that Peter and John
defied the civil authorities when they were told not to preach.
They informed the authorities when they would have to judge
whether the apostles should obey God or men. The apostles
continued to preach. Many people have inferred from this that
if a believer in Christ thinks a particular law is unjust it should
be ignored. That is not what this Scripture passage is saying.
Actually in this case Peter emphasized subjection to the boss.
The case in Acts was different: Peter and John were commanded by public authorities not to do something the public
law allowed them to do. The law was being misrepresented.
When he had to differ with them Peter humbly said he would
have to differ, because he knew the law.

There was no law against a man speaking for God among the
Jewish people. When Peter and John did speak for God, one
might say they disregarded the wishes of the rulers. I do not
think they disobeyed God. When they were punished, Peter
and John went out of the presence of the council rejoicing that
they were counted worthy to suffer shame for His name. They
bought their liberty to preach and paid for it, and made no
objection. That is a different story. In this passage we are
talking about doing a piece of work or being hired out to a boss
who tells his servant what to do, and the servant does it.

Perhaps the boss does not treat you right, but you still remain humble. Peter leaves no doubt as to what God's word would be: "Be subject to your own master with all fear." This means the believer should appropriately respect and treat his boss with courtesy, not only the good boss, but also the froward boss, the man who is not good. God lets believers have experiences very much like training experiences. The suffering that believers endure enables them to act in such a way that God would be pleased.

> For what glory is it, if, when ye be buffeted for your faults, ye shall take it patiently? but if, when ye do well, and suffer for it, ye take it patiently, this is acceptable with God (1 Peter 2:20).

How hard it is, humanly speaking, to see that, and yet how very important this principle is. We wonder whether this is the true dynamic of living in Christ. Is this really what believers in Christ should be seeking? They should live in such a way as to win the approval of their Father in heaven. Is this what believers really ought to do? Apparently this is possible only for such as believe there is a promise of reward.

CHRIST LEFT AN EXAMPLE
(1 Peter 2:21-23)

Do you realize that Christ Jesus left only one example to guide His followers?

> For even hereunto were ye called: because Christ also suffered for us, leaving us an example, that ye should follow his steps: who did no sin, neither was guile found in his mouth: who, when he was reviled, reviled not again; when he suffered, he threatened not; but committed himself to him that judgeth righteously (1 Peter 2:21-23).

Here is the outstanding example that Christ Jesus left for His followers. What some people do not realize is that Jesus of Nazareth provided for only one aspect of life, and that was not an example of how to live. The example was how to die. Almost anyone, hearing about Jesus, is ready to think He went around showing how things were to be done. But this is not to be found in the New Testament. There is only one thing He performed that His followers could do, and He did that as an example: He washed the disciples' feet. He did leave believers an example in what He did when He offered Himself to die.

To the cross of Calvary is the one short route in which believers can follow the Lord Jesus Christ. Some would make it appear that any human being can manage to please God if he will humbly be patient when he is suffering; he would then be following the steps of Jesus. This is subtle, and not quite true. Any time, anywhere, in any given situation a believer can follow His steps in that he can die: dying unto self; yielding himself to die. For example, a woman who is having difficulties in her home can reckon herself, indeed, to be dead. When she counts herself dead, but alive in Christ Jesus, Christ will keep the house. This can happen when the woman lets the Holy Spirit of God dwell in her.

"For even hereunto were ye called: because Christ also suffered for us." Suffering is what God has in mind for believers, and suffering at the hands of careless persons can apparently be in the plan of God. "Christ also suffered for us," leaving us an example. Those who made Jesus of Nazareth suffer were not worthy people, and often those who mistreat believers in Christ are also unworthy. Christ was reviled, yet He reviled not again. If believers follow Him, serving faithfully and humbly, it is entirely possible they will suffer crucifixion the way He did. Remember, the only thing He showed believers to do was to take the flesh to the cross. This is the point in these verses we have been considering.

DELIVERANCE BY CHRIST
(1 Peter 2:24-25)

Do you realize Christ Jesus did something on Calvary's cross that affects every believer in his daily life?

> Who his own self bare our sins in his own body on the tree, that
> we, being dead to sins, should live unto righteousness: by whose

stripes ye were healed. For ye were as sheep going astray; but
are now returned unto the Shepherd and Bishop of your souls
(1 Peter 2:24-25).

Those of us who know about the Gospel understand that
people can be saved by the blood of Jesus Christ, yet many
times we stop short in our understanding. What does it mean
when we say, "Who his own self bare our sins in his own body
on the tree, that we, being dead to sins should live unto
righteousness"? When you received Jesus Christ, what did
you do? Did you agree to a proposition? In this statement it
could be assumed that Christ's death paid the fine and you are
free.

To be saved means not only that believers are saved from
condemnation to hell, which they are, but it means that they
are saved from the bondage of sin. We read in the second
statement, "By whose stripes we were healed." Not that believers are "going" to be healed; they actually were healed. We
all know what it is to be vaccinated against smallpox. What
happens is that someone had smallpox and the blood of that
particular person is changed so it has the ability to destroy the
smallpox germ. In vaccination, some of this changed blood is
injected into a person's blood. His blood system is then able to
overcome smallpox. When a person receives Jesus Christ
something like this seems to be the case. Jesus of Nazareth
gained the victory over sin by dying in the flesh. That is what
the phrase "by his stripes" means. When a person receives
Him by faith, he receives Christ into his own consciousness.
The victory that Christ achieved gets into the system and that
person receives the capacity to deal with sin. Believers do not
die physically at that time, but something of the Lord Jesus
Christ, who did die physically, gets into the spiritual blood
stream and sets the believers free. That is how believers are
saved from their sin. In that sense believers, being dead to sin
because they are dead in Jesus Christ, should live unto righteousness.

"For ye were as sheep going astray; but are now returned
unto the Shepherd and Bishop of your souls." To be as sheep
going astray means everyone would go his own way. That is
something the Lord Jesus did not do. He could say, "I do
always the things that please my Father." When a person

receives Jesus Christ into his heart there follows the disposition to always obey the Father. "Christ in you" inspires the believer into the will of God. With His Spirit within their hearts, believers seek the face of God. It is not so much that a believer turns away from evil, as it is that a believer turns to God. This turns him away from evil.

FIRST PETER
Chapter 3

✝ ✝ ✝

HOW COULD THE WIFE WIN THE HUSBAND?
(1 Peter 3:1-2)

Do you know what a wife can do to win her husband to the Lord when he does not want to hear one word about religion?

> Likewise, ye wives, be in subjection to your own husbands; that, if any obey not the word, they also may without the word be won by the conversation of the wives; while they behold your chaste conversation coupled with fear (1 Peter 3:1-2).

Notice that first word, "likewise"; hold to it. Now turn again to verses 18 to 25 in the second chapter. Everything written to servants is "likewise" to apply to wives, and for the same reason. We often miss the idea, as far as the believer's experience is concerned, that suffering is necessary. We do not want to suffer, and the promises of God are gracious and merciful. "Come unto me and I will give you rest." We want that rest. In that call the suffering was already implied as the weariness and heavy laden part. "In the world you shall have tribulation." "Man is born to trouble as the sparks fly upward." When one becomes a believer in Christ, he might feel that he will escape trouble. It is true a believer can escape trouble, after he has been to Calvary. It is always a classic procedure: first, the cross; then, the crown. Then we shall have peace. If a believer yields himself unto death he will come into peace. The peace of God that passeth all understanding will keep his mind and heart in Christ Jesus.

This is not sinister or strange. We may try to ignore it. Many times we talk about everything being sweet and lovely, as though there will be no trouble. When trouble comes we begin to think we are not true believers, or that God is not keeping His word, or that someone did not lead us right. But this is not true. Are you going to walk with the Lord? Then remember how the Lord walked: for Him it meant going to the cross. It is important for you to be patient as a believer in Christ, especially when you are being unjustly treated. "When he was reviled, he reviled not again."

"Likewise, ye wives be in subjection to your own husbands." For a wife to be in subjection does not mean that she is inferior. The whole meaning of the word "wife," from Eve to the present time, is that she is to be a helper to her husband. This subjection is an administrative term. Being in subjection is not because he is better than she; it is because he is leading and she is following. She accepts his leadership. This calls for real humility; it is not abject fear but a wholesome respect, not so much because the man is worth it, but because this is the practical arrangement.

"If any obey not the word," if he is not responsive to the call of God, "they also may without the word be won by the conversation of the wives." Apart from anything the woman might say, he might be won. That does not say he is saved. "Won" does not mean saved; he could be won to a favorable attitude so that he would consider the Gospel and look to the Lord. The Lord will save the man but the wife could win him. He would be won by his wife's manner of life. This manner of life on the part of the wife does not focus so much upon her husband. It is not the wife's attitude toward her husband, but the wife's attitude toward her own ego. "While they behold your chaste conversation coupled with fear," they notice your humble self-denial; your humility; your reverence toward God; your respect toward man; and your regard for the poor. These things speak for themselves to everybody—even to the husband.

THE BELIEVING WOMAN'S APPEARANCE
(1 Peter 3:3-6)

Do you think there is necessarily anything wrong when a woman is conscious of her appearance and wants to look nice in the eyes of others?

> Whose adorning let it not be that outward adorning of plaiting the hair, and of wearing of gold, or of putting on of apparel; but let it be the hidden man of the heart, in that which is not corruptible, even the ornament of a meek and quiet spirit, which is in the sight of God of great price. For after this manner in the old time the holy women also, who trusted in God, adorned themselves, being in subjection unto their own husbands: even as Sarah obeyed Abraham, calling him lord: whose daughters ye are, as long as ye do well, and are not afraid with any amazement (1 Peter 3:3-6).

The matter of adornment or of appearance is a natural thing for anybody, and especially for a woman; and it is very healthy. We can often tell the condition of a woman's general frame of mind, and certainly her morale, when we consider her interest in her appearance. For a believing woman, interest in her appearance need not be a matter of vanity; it can be consideration of others. It can also definitely be a matter of self-respect because, in that way, a woman can treat herself in a way that shows she respects herself.

It is natural for anyone with this much interest in appearance to feel comparison with others. And comparison with others, even though it is natural, can be dangerous. That does not make it evil. Eating a large meal can be dangerous; but that does not make it evil. It is quite normal for one to wish to appear favorable in comparison with others. It is not always necessary to look better than others, but one would not want to look worse. Adorning in itself is not evil, and Peter did not mean to say that it is. "Let it not be that outward adorning of plaiting the hair and of wearing of gold, or of putting on of apparel." Peter emphasized that as far as appearance is concerned, it should not depend upon the beauty parlor, nor upon jewelry and dress.

The appearance of a woman's face and hair, or her ornaments and her dress, are much like money. A number of people feel that money is an evil thing, believing that the Bible teaches money is evil. This is an error. The Bible says the "love" of money is the "root" of all evil. Money can be dangerous. Just so the love of adornments can be evil. Because of this, some people will not use jewelry of any kind, or hairdressing at all. We have great respect for those who have convictions along this line. At the same time, I must make this observation: if one bases his understanding upon this passage of Scripture, and one believes that Peter wrote a believer should not plait the hair and put on any kind of gold, one should look further. Look at what else he says about putting on apparel. A person does not have to wear an old, out-of-style dress in order to be a true believer. We are told here we should not "depend" upon these things. When the believer in Christ comes into the presence of other people, she should look as inconspicuous as possible; she should wear something that is modest. It is best not to criticize others, nor to judge them, when they wear whatever is modish.

Peter wrote further, "The ornament of a meek and quiet spirit, which is in the sight of God of great price." "Meek": having no resentment. "A quiet spirit": no loud seeking attention; this is a pearl of great price. Peter went on, "For after this manner in the old time the holy women also, who trusted in God, adorned themselves, being in subjection unto their own husbands." Women have always been interested in their appearance, but holy women adorned themselves with this ornament of a meek and quiet spirit. Truly there is something in the old proverb, "Handsome is as handsome does." Peter wrote that in all these things a woman will conduct herself in such a way that her husband will feel a sense of appreciation for her. Even Sarah did this when she obeyed Abraham, "calling him lord; whose daughters ye are, as long as ye do well, and are not afraid with any amazement."

That last phrase means that a woman need not give herself over to anxieties or to hysterical fears. She should put her trust in the Lord.

HOW A HUSBAND SHOULD TREAT HIS WIFE
(1 Peter 3:7)

Do you think it makes any difference in a man's spiritual experience as to how he treats his wife?

> Likewise, ye husbands, dwell with them according to knowledge, giving honour unto the wife, as unto the weaker vessel, and as being heirs together of the grace of life; that your prayers be not hindered (1 Peter 3:7).

Our attention is here focused on husbands. There is only one verse, but it says much to believing men. It would be helpful for anyone, but we have no expectation that it will affect people who are not yielded to the Lord. The word "likewise" indicates that just as servants were to endure suffering because it was in the will of God, so wives are to endure suffering in being subject to their husbands. In the plan of God being a good servant will include passing through experiences that require self-denial, even to self-crucifixion.

"Dwell with them according to knowledge." Dwelling with them may need interpretation, but it is real. The husband is to share with his wife. How many problems would be solved if husband and wife "lived" together! Responsibility rests upon the man because he has the opportunity; if he did not want to take her, she could not force herself on him.

"Giving honor unto the wife, as unto the weaker vessel." It is true that the average man is physically stronger than the average woman. She may be able to endure suffering more than he, but most men can lift a bigger load, taking the rough side of activity when it needs to be done.

God promised blessings, ". . . as being heirs together of the grace of life." Here Peter meant that if the man acts like a gentleman, he will be acting like a true believer in Christ.

"That your prayers be not hindered." Paul wrote to husbands they should not be bitter against their wives (Col. 3:19). He meant they should be forgiving. God will not bless a cruel person or a selfish person. Peter here emphasized the same truth.

CONDUCT BETWEEN BELIEVERS
(1 Peter 3:8-9)

Do you realize how important it is for a believer in Christ to be courteous?

> Finally, be ye all of one mind, having compassion one of another, love as brethren, be pitiful, be courteous: not rendering evil for evil, or railing for railing: but contrariwise blessing; knowing that ye are thereunto called, that ye should inherit a blessing (1 Peter 3:8-9).

I am sure Peter wrote these messages so that believing people would know how to get along together. He outlined the various ways the believer should act in order to receive blessing. In chapter 2 verse 11 he told the believers as strangers and pilgrims to "abstain from fleshly lusts which war against the soul." This means much more than just a few evil desires. Peter raised the question with them, did they want to be blessed? They should abstain from fleshly lusts. They should deny self by humbly submitting to the demands of various situations. "Finally, be ye all of one mind." This is very demanding. In order for a number of people to be of one mind they would have to be humble, self-controlled, and in agreement.

It is not possible for believers to be of one mind unless they deny some aspects of their own ideas. If three or more are together, they will have to deny self more. This is the general principle. "Having compassion one with another," this is what it takes to be of one mind. "Love as brethren," care for each other as if they belonged to each other. "Be pitiful," some of the brethren are lacking in some of the better traits. Believers are to be full of pity so far as such are concerned. "Be courteous," which is far more than good manners or being polite. Being polite is an outward way of doing things, a matter of policy, but courtesy is doing something that will please the other person. The believer should start fellowship with a cheerful smile. Not everyone feels like smiling all the time. Some persons can smile for your sake in order to make you feel better. This is the function of a believer; and it is involved in receiving the blessing of God. This is what it means to be of one mind. "Not rendering evil for evil." There will be evil. Some things that happen are not good. There will be quarreling, criticism, and at times sarcasm. The believer should not retaliate; he should be gracious to others so that he might be blessed. If the believer will treat people graciously, God will treat him graciously. "Knowing that ye are thereunto called, that ye should inherit a blessing."

How would you like to have God treat you? You should treat the other person just like that and God will bless you.

THE BELIEVER'S CONDUCT MATTERS TO GOD
(1 Peter 3:10-12)

Did you know that it makes a difference to God how a believer in Christ acts among other men?

> For he that will love life, and see good days, let him refrain his tongue from evil, and his lips that they speak no guile: let him eschew evil, and do good; let him seek peace, and ensue it. For the eyes of the Lord are over the righteous, and his ears are open unto their prayers: but the face of the Lord is against them that do evil (1 Peter 3:10-12).

After a person becomes a believer and receives Jesus Christ as Savior, committing self to Him, God sends His Holy Spirit into the believer's heart. The believer then has the grace of God operative in his life when he needs it. It is something like this: if a person wants to have a garden he will need land. After he obtains the land, he needs to work to have a garden. In the same way, if a man wants to have a home, he will get married; and then, as Edgar Guest once wrote, "It takes a heap of living in a house to make it a home." Willingness to work is included in living the life of a believer. The blessing of God is wonderful, worth every effort on our part.

If you want a garden you get the land and work it; you plant the seed and cultivate and irrigate it. Then you will have a garden. So it is with reference to the blessing of God, "For he that will love life, and see good days, let him refrain his tongue from evil, and his lips that they speak no guile." Is it not strange that Peter should start with a man's tongue? We use the tongue not only to talk, but also to think. It is what we think as well as what we say that is important. The believer should carefully edit his words; he should control his thoughts. "Let him eschew evil, and do good." To eschew evil is to leave it alone. The believer should not be unkind; that is wrong. He should not be thoughtless about other people; that is wrong. It may cost something to do good in the presence of others who do not do good, but if the believer wants blessing, he must do good. "Seek peace and ensue it." One may wonder how to seek peace. The procedure is simple; he must let go and give. Many of us do not want to do this because we are afraid that if we do not hold what we have we may lose it. If we do not take care of ourselves something will happen to hurt us. Believers should trust God! Walk righteously in His sight. Believers should work on these things.

"For the eyes of the Lord are over the righteous, and his ears are open unto their prayers." Believers should remember His eyes are upon them; "But the face of the Lord is against them that do evil." When a person believes in the Lord Jesus Christ, Christ will put into his heart the will to walk with God; and God will walk with him.

CONDUCT BEFORE UNBELIEVERS
(1 Peter 3:13-15)

Do you realize that a believer in Christ can suffer ill treatment from other people simply because they do not understand him?

> And who is he that will harm you, if ye be followers of that which is good? But and if ye suffer for righteousness' sake, happy are ye: and be not afraid of their terror, neither be troubled; but sanctify the Lord God in your hearts: and be ready always to give an answer to every man that asketh you a reason of the hope that is in you with meekness and fear (1 Peter 3:13-15).

Here Peter began to direct the thinking of the believers along a new line. He wants to guide believers in their public relation with other people. Peter takes up the matter of the treatment other people will give the believer. A believer in Christ has no reason to fear that anyone will mistreat him. There is really no reason why they should. A believer in Christ does nobody harm. A believer in Christ works for the good of everybody, yet strangely enough there will be opposition; often ill-will. There will be those who do not like him because they do not like what he represents. There are unreasonable and wicked men. Paul says in one place, "All men have not faith." Peter dealt with this: "If ye suffer for righteousness' sake, happy are ye." Believers should not let anything frighten them; they are representing God. "But sanctify the Lord God in your hearts." This is an unusual expression. In their thinking, they should give God His praise; honor Him. Some will oppose believers and believers will have their inward feelings. Peter urged them to remember God and put their trust in Him. He would take care of them.

When the three Hebrews in the Book of Daniel were threatened with being put into the fiery furnace it did not seem to upset them. When the king asked if God could save them from the fiery furnace they answered:

> Our God whom we serve is able to deliver us from the burning fiery furnace, and he will deliver us out of thine hand, O king (Dan. 3:17).

The believer should remember he is standing in God's presence, and then, "Be ready always to give an answer to every man that asketh you a reason of the hope that is in you with meekness and fear." This would be the hope that God will take care of him. "With meekness and fear." The word "meekness" implies primarily the idea of no resentment. Even though they have been mistreated, there will be no resentment on their part. "Fear" is respect; they are to act courteously and respectfully. The believers should treat their persecutors graciously, kindly, and tell them the truth. Such men do not deserve this, but the truth is a bit like this: even in the dark, a diamond will sparkle. If the believer has real faith, it must shine, even in the dark.

THE BELIEVER'S GOOD TESTIMONY
(1 Peter 3:16)

Would you understand that the most practical way a believer in Christ can be guided is through his conscience?

> Having a good conscience; that, whereas they speak evil of you, as of evildoers, they may be ashamed that falsely accuse your good conversation in Christ (1 Peter 3:16).

The Holy Spirit has been given to believers to guide them daily. They do not have to face life alone. Even with this provision of the guidance of the Holy Spirit there can be doubts in matters of judgment. A believer cannot always be sure he is doing the wise thing. Now the Holy Spirit can incline him to want to do the will of God, but what is the will of God? The Holy Spirit can move the believer so that the believer wants to honor the Lord Jesus Christ. But "what" will honor the Lord Jesus Christ? Sometimes the answer will be found in prayer, but there is not always time for this research in prayer.

God has given another means to guide the believer: his conscience. But the conscience that God has given to him is not nearly as significant as the Holy Spirit. Yet the conscience is very helpful, and Peter makes use of it here. If we put good conscience and good "conversation" together (by the way, the word "conversation" means manner of life), we could say conscience is derived to a certain extent from the life of the group. In this sense the form of conscience is of social origin. People's consciences vary. If a person grew up in a certain community among a certain class of people he would have a certain type of conscience that would point in a certain direction. A person has a good conscience when he does what he considers to be good. One person could live in one country and have a good conscience acting in a certain way, but someone in another country would not have a good conscience unless he acted in a different way.

There are churches where all of the men sit on one side of the sanctuary; all of the women sit on the other side. If a man comes in with his wife and she sits with the women while he sits with the men, he could do this with a good conscience. In the church I attend, if a husband sat separated from his wife he might not have a good conscience. This illustration indicates that conscience will guide one in matters of choice. There would be no question about conscience when something like stealing were involved. Killing people and lying are wrong in most societies.

The matter of conscience is involved in the manner in which one conducts self: what is said under certain circumstances, what is done under certain circumstances. A person has a good conscience when he does not act against his good judgment; he would have a bad conscience if he did go against it. Conscience will make you aware of what you are doing, and will accuse or excuse you. Nobody has a good conscience naturally, but a person "can" have one.

> How much more shall the blood of Christ, who through the eternal Spirit offered himself without spot to God, purge your conscience from dead works to serve the living God? (Heb. 9:14).

When a person becomes a believer in Christ his conscience becomes a better conscience, a purged conscience, which guides him. He feels led to do that which is right. "Having a good conscience; that, whereas they speak evil of you, as of evildoers, they may be ashamed that falsely accuse your good conversation in Christ." He will have a good way of living in Christ Jesus when he keeps a good conscience; doing what he believes is right.

"Speak evil of you"—this will happen. It is a natural reaction. When the apostle Paul came into the city of Jerusalem and was arrested there, he was accused of stirring up an insurrection, causing a rebellion. Standing in court he said:

> Neither can they prove the things whereof they now accuse me. But this I confess unto thee, that after the way which they call heresy, so worship I the God of my fathers, believing all things which are written in the law and in the prophets: and have hope toward God, which they themselves also allow, that there shall be a resurrection of the dead, both of the just and unjust. And herein do I exercise myself, to have always a conscience void of offense toward God, and toward men (Acts 24:13-16).

When Mary was anointing the feet of Jesus of Nazareth, Judas criticized her. He spoke evil of her. On another occasion even her sister, Martha, spoke unkindly of her. It is not unusual for people to criticize believers, but Peter wrote that if the believer has a good conscience and they speak evil of him, they will be ashamed when they see his manner of life. Having a good conscience includes an element of choice on your part: an element of being committed to. This good conscience will guide the believer into such deeds and good works, that these will speak for themselves. If a believer will simply act the way he feels inwardly led, he will not have to make a spiritual occasion of each instance. He can act as a matter of course.

The believer shows reverence toward God; he will attend church; he will read the Bible and respect the Sabbath day. Everybody who sees him will know him. He will respect those in authority; he will share in all good works. He will have regard for others and be a good neighbor. When the believer does these things people cannot talk against him; and this is what Peter is saying.

THE MEANING OF SUFFERING
(1 Peter 3:17-18)

Do you realize that a believer in Christ may suffer even when he is doing well?

> For it is better, if the will of God be so, that ye suffer for well doing, than for evil doing. For Christ also hath once suffered for sins, the just for the unjust, that he might bring us to God, being put to death in the flesh, but quickened by the Spirit (1 Peter 3:17-18).

No one wants to suffer. Perhaps of all the human experiences we have, there is one upon which we all agree and that is we do not want to be hurting. Strain is hard; hurt is painful; bruises are hard to bear. One cannot endure hunger; thirst is indescribable. It seems that the human being, constituted as he is, can hurt in many different ways, and pain is common to man. Pleasure is desirable, and people will do much to feel a little gladness about anything. Some pain is accidental. Some pain is eventual; it happens because of what is done. Some pain is incidental: we have it in order to arrive at something; e.g. the pain of doing homework in order to get the assignment done. One may have pain at times in going through the tedium of preparing a meal in order that people may eat. Some pain is caused by others and this is, in many ways, the most unbearable kind. But there is no way to escape some suffering.

As we study these verses we see that Peter suggests we bring our suffering into our relationship with God, and fit it into our spiritual experience. Apparently suffering is not universal. We do not suffer every day or in everything. It is not constant. It is not automatic. Some have suffered much. Some have suffered in heart, having had real trouble; some have suffered in body, having physical aches and pains. The believer should remember that God has His hand upon him. Peter would urge him to put his trust in God. The believer should sanctify the Lord God in his heart. He should walk closely with God.

A believer in Christ has some prerogative when it comes to this matter of suffering, some choice of which way to go. Here again Peter would tell him to go the good way and do the good thing. The believer could then expect a blessing of God. In this the believer would be following the example of Jesus Christ, who went about doing good always. In His doing good and suffering, He actually suffered for other people who had done wrong: "For Christ also hath once suffered for sins, the just for the unjust." He had not sinned yet He suffered on account of the sins of others, "that he might bring us to God, being put to death in the flesh, but quickened by the Spirit." Peter referred to this over and over again and believers must not lose sight of it.

The entire Gospel story emphasizes the idea that believers are to die in the flesh and be made alive in the Spirit. Christ Jesus Himself, suffering for sins, died in the flesh that He might be made alive by the Spirit. Believers have that example. The believer in Christ can accept his own suffering as a means to glory, understanding that this suffering is working a greater glory for those who trust in the Lord Jesus Christ. The suffering that you endure patiently now can actually be made to bring certain blessed consequences in the future.

Some would be willing to suffer if it meant that one dear to them would become a believer in Christ, but it is not altogether like that, although it is not entirely separate from it. It is quite possible that if a believer will patiently endure and keep turning to God at all times, he may bring those for whom he cares to God. Jesus of Nazareth had no sins of His own but He suffered for the sins of others. It is possible that a believer may be suffering because of the sins of others. In that case he could pray about it, and ask Almighty God to accept his suffering on their behalf, and to be gracious and to turn them unto Himself.

In the case of a believer who has his own sins, he could accept the suffering as self-induced suffering; as the self-induced pain caused by sin. This would not be payment, but suffering in the way of dying; like seeds fall into the ground and die that they might bring forth fruit. In that sense a believer could accept suffering as a way in which the flesh is actually done to death in order that the spirit can live. The believer could accept the suffering he has as being caused by sin, but in that very suffering the Son of God in him can redeem him from death into life. The formula is that the believer is put to death in the flesh but quickened by the Spirit.

Let us keep in mind that if suffering has to do with the consequences of sin, that is what we have in the flesh. If we will put our trust in God when we suffer, it will not be in vain. As surely as we suffer in the flesh He will raise us from the dead and we can live in the Spirit to the glory of God.

SALVATION MEANS LIVING IN CHRIST
(1 Peter 3:19-20)

Is it clear to you the Bible teaches that disobedience will bring about destruction?

> By which also he went and preached unto the spirits in prison; which sometime were disobedient, when once the long-suffering of God waited in the days of Noah, while the ark was a preparing, wherein few, that is, eight souls were saved by water (1 Peter 3:19-20).

It is not unusual for people to think that the grace of God is universal. Everyone will have it; it will come regardless. It is easy to think that God will do only good to people, and no one will ever be hurt, or in trouble. Some would have you think that God is responsible for deciding who will believe. However, the Bible seems to indicate that God says, "Whosoever will may come." It seems equally clear that the truth of God's grace as seen in Christ Jesus is to be preached to all men everywhere as a call, and whosoever will call upon the name of the Lord shall be saved. Bear in mind that the operation of the grace of God in the Gospel of Jesus Christ needs to be preached.

As we look into this passage, ". . . the spirits in prison" could refer to persons in their sinful flesh. I think those are the spirits in prison; they are in bondage to sin. When Jesus of Nazareth was here He told the people that He had come to set the prisoners free. When we think of the spirits being in prison we are thinking of the spirit being not able or free to do as he will. This is the case of man in his sin. "Which sometime were disobedient." Could this mean that God preached through the flood back in the days of Noah? Was He preaching to the spirits that were in prison; those who were involved in sinful flesh even then?

What did the flood actually say? That the world which then was could not endure; that it must be destroyed; but that people could be saved? Safety was only for those who repudiated the world that then was, and took refuge in the ark which God prepared. Is this not the same message today?

We read that Noah was a preacher of righteousness for 120 years while the ark was being built. While he was building the ark the message was going forth constantly. The fact that Noah was building the ark implied to everybody that Noah thought there would be a flood that would destroy all of them, but they did not believe it. It was not Noah's idea to preach; it was God's. This was the message of the second person of the Godhead, even back in those days before He became incarnate, preaching to the people of the world at that time.

The world as it is will not survive. Man needs to be rescued, delivered; and God delivered those eight people who were in the ark. Even though the reference may be obscure, the Gospel is indicated clearly. "For Christ also hath once suffered for sins, the just for the unjust, that he might bring us to God,

being put to death in the flesh, but quickened by the Spirit"
(1 Peter 3:18). God preached to those people, telling them that
God would not sustain the world they were living in. The world
would be destroyed but all who would get into the ark would be
saved. Only eight persons in all went into the ark, and they
were saved. Surely this is God preaching, the second person of
the Godhead. Here is the great truth that is in creation and in
salvation: the first creation (human nature) cannot inherit the
Kingdom of God. It will never be eternally sustained; it must
die. Then it can be raised from the dead into newness of life
and have the blessing of God.

SAVED BY THE RESURRECTION OF CHRIST
(1 Peter 3:21-22)

Can you understand that baptism is not so much washing
away the sins of the flesh as it is bringing the believer into the
will of Jesus Christ?

Even among believing people it is easy, in trying to understand the Gospel, to stop short of the whole truth. Perhaps
unconsciously, when we think about the things of the Lord, we
tend to think only of what people generally say. Here we could
easily be hindered, because many may discuss the Gospel, but
have not yet fully received Christ. They believe He is the Son
of God; they believe everything that is said about Him, but
they have not received this for themselves. Yet they talk about
it. It is obvious they cannot possibly understand what they are
talking about.

In presenting the Gospel, attention is usually centered upon
sin. When people first hear the Gospel they think about their
sin and its penalty. And truly here the Gospel shines brightly.
Christ Jesus died for our sins and this is marvelously true, but
this is not the full Gospel. He rose again the third day. Sometimes I wonder if the death of Christ should be preached
without mentioning the resurrection. Is it not written with
reference to His accepting the cross, "Who for the joy that was
set before him endured the cross" (Heb. 12:2)? What was the

joy? Was it the joy of dying? Oh, no. He had His eyes on the recompense of the reward.

The Gospel is implied in this simple statement: He died to live. Notice how this is emphasized in First Peter 3:21-22. He has just spoken about how preaching was done to the spirits in prison at the time of Noah.

> The like figure whereunto even baptism doth also now save us (not the putting away of the filth of the flesh, but the answer of a good conscience toward God,) by the resurrection of Jesus Christ: who is gone into heaven, and is on the right hand of God; angels and authorities and powers being made subject unto him (1 Peter 3:21-22).

You can get the whole meaning of the sentence in verse 21 if you read that baptism even now also doth save us by the resurrection of Jesus Christ. Peter puts in the explanatory clause: "Not the putting away of the filth of the flesh, but the answer of a good conscience toward God." Now putting away of the filth of the flesh means simply washing away the dirt from sin. Washing away the filth of sin is part of baptism but not all, and not the main part of it. We are being led to yield ourselves to the Lord Jesus Christ in baptism, knowing that the sins will be taken away; but also that we will be made alive in Him. The washing away of sins is included, but serving in the newness of life is the main emphasis.

Almost everyone knows about the flood, and I suspect many have thought of the flood as a judgment; and that is what it was. The flood came because of sin. That is partly true, but not altogether so. The significance of the flood is in the ark that saved Noah. The flood destroyed the sinful world in order that Noah might be saved from it. Jesus Christ died in the flesh so that my flesh, with its sinfulness, might die, and that I might live in Christ Jesus, free from the sinfulness of my flesh. This is the marvelous truth. The death of the flesh is involved in salvation, but living in the spirit is salvation. That is the other side. The "putting away of the filth of the flesh" is not the main thing, but the answer of a good conscience, which we read about in verses 11, 12, and 13. That is the significance of being in Christ. We are baptized not only into His death but into His resurrection. Death is for once, but resurrection is forever.

This Jesus Christ "Who is gone into heaven" (verse 22) died

for me; He bore my sins in His own body on the tree. He is alive now, bringing us into the presence of God. Let us rejoice in it. "And is on the right hand of God." That is the believer's place now. He died for us and we joined Him on the cross, in order that being raised from the dead we might join Him in the presence of God. "Angels and authorities and powers being made subject unto him."

Believers in Christ Jesus can live in the victory that is in Jesus Christ as their Head of the body, living now in heaven at the right hand of God, overruling all things. That will is now activated in the believer. This is the wonderful truth of salvation that Peter brings to us. Believers can thank God their sins are forgiven, and praise Him that they can live in Christ forever.

FIRST PETER

Chapter 4

✝   ✝   ✝

BELIEVERS SUFFER THAT THEY MAY SERVE
(1 Peter 4:1-2)

Would you understand that living as a believer in Christ means living a different kind of life?

> Forasmuch then as Christ hath suffered for us in the flesh, arm yourselves likewise with the same mind: for he that hath suffered in the flesh hath ceased from sin; that he no longer should live the rest of his time in the flesh to the lusts of men, but to the will of God (1 Peter 4:1-2).

To be a believer in Christ is to be different. Some might say that going to church makes one different; but people go to church for many different reasons: some to meet friends, some to be with family, or to find customers or prospects. Others go to worship God, to hear His Word and praise His Son. These are the valid reasons; not natural reasons. Being a believer in Christ means to live differently. The way to be a believer in Christ is to die in the flesh, and to be born again so as to live in the Spirit. We remember the words of the Lord Jesus Christ:

> If any man will come after me, let him deny himself, and take up his cross, and follow me (Matt. 16:24).

Paul could speak of having done this when he said:

> I am crucified with Christ: nevertheless I live; yet not I, but Christ liveth in me: and the life which I now live in the flesh I live by the faith of the Son of God, who loved me, and gave himself for me (Gal. 2:20).

On the one hand is the matter of dying in the flesh, and on the other hand is the matter of living in the Spirit, that which has to do with God. This is not reasonable to the carnal mind; it is about Christ, not about self.

One big point then, in being a Christian, is that the believer dies. He denies himself unto death in the flesh that he might live in the Spirit as a member of the body of Christ. This is what we read in First Peter 4:1. Suffering for us "in the flesh" meant going through Gethsemane and through Calvary. Forasmuch as Christ has done this for us, "arm yourselves likewise" (prepare yourself for the battle; get ready in the same way with the same mind; be ready to die) "for he that hath suffered in the flesh has ceased from sin." This suffering in the flesh does not mean that the believer has headaches or similar ailments. This means a person who has suffered in Christ's crucifixion, who has shared with Him in denying self. According to Romans 6, if the flesh is once dead, this means the flesh which was enmeshed in sin is dead and believers are free from it. This is not so much a report of what has happened in events, as it is the description of a new situation.

After Calvary comes the grave. Once the believer decides against selfishness, self-indulgence, self-praise, let him bury these. "That he no longer should live the rest of his time in the flesh to the lusts of men, but to the will of God." If the believer can do with or without a particular thing, he should do without it. There will be things to do as led by the Holy Spirit, if believers are not too busy trying to please other people.

BELIEVERS LIVE DIFFERENTLY
(1 Peter 4:3-6)

Do you realize there are people all around you who are not affected by God?

> For the time past of our life may suffice us to have wrought the will of the Gentiles, when we walked in lasciviousness, lusts, excess of wine, revellings, banquetings, and abominable idolatries: wherein they think it strange that ye run not with them to the same excess of riot, speaking evil of you (1 Peter 4:3-4).

As I pointed out in our last study, being a believer in Christ is not so much a difference in what a person does, as it is a real difference in his inward motivation. It is customary to say when a person is a follower of Christ that he can do with or without anything. He can go on a boat ride or he can stay at home. Peter would say in this connection that if he could get along with drinking beer or without drinking it, he should not drink it. If he can get along with the use of tobacco or without it, he should get along without it. The time is here now when the believer can very wisely withdraw from the activities of other human beings, so that he may have more time for the things of God. This is brought out clearly in 4:3-6.

Here in verse 3 is Peter's own personal testimony when he wrote that he had done enough of the popular things that pleased the people. The language used is rather formal and many of us may think it does not refer to us, in which case we have not understood it. Whatever was going on back in those days is going on in our day. Walking in lasciviousness would be in sensuality, doing things according to feelings. In some cases this would be with shameless and insolent wantonness. Lusts mean strong desires; they can be good and bad. I will use here the word "addiction."

It is easy to tell to what a person is addicted; what does he spend his money on? It could be excessive wine or tobacco. Is there anything he does that is indulgent in nature? Does he spend money on certain things in an excessive manner? This does not mean these things need be bad in themselves, but just that he spends too much money on them. What are the things that engage his whole attention? Pleasure jaunts, outings, beach parties? Peter once did this kind of thing. You may say: these are not bad. That is like saying that weeds growing in a garden are not bad. As for "abominable idolatries," no one will think he does anything like that, because he does not worship heathen idols or forbidden gods. But do you participate in big football expeditions or big homecoming affairs at the university? What Peter is saying is that if a believer is doing any of these various things to excess, he should let that go. He should lay them away.

"Wherein they think it strange that ye run not with them to the same excess of riot, speaking evil of you." Some will not understand why the believer does not share with them in their activities. If such are relatives or friends, they will criticize the believer. Peter says these people shall give account to Him that is ready to judge the quick and the dead. Now the quick are those who are alive, having been raised from the dead; quickened unto life. The dead are those who are dead in trespasses and sin.

> For for this cause was the gospel preached also to them that are dead, that they might be judged according to men in the flesh, but live according to God in the spirit (1 Peter 4:6).

The same straightforward presentation of the Gospel preaches the truth of God in such a way that it judges the sins of the flesh. In the sight of Gospel preaching, one can feel what a sinner he is. But it also shows that the believer can live with God in the spirit, and it offers the grace of God for living in Christ Jesus. Peter urged in view of all these things: let believers turn away from those things that appeal to the flesh, and let them yield themselves to God.

BELIEVERS SOBERLY PRAY FOR HELP
(1 Peter 4:7)

Do you think anybody ever realizes how serious life really is?

> But the end of all things is at hand: be ye therefore sober, and watch unto prayer (1 Peter 4:7).

Here Peter sums up what he has been talking about in the first three chapters. When he says, "The end of all things is at hand," he means that time has come for the showdown. We are now where it really counts. "Be ye therefore sober" means be serious-minded; do not be flighty about things. Do not be imaginative about things. Be practical and think seriously. Let there be no wishful thinking. One should not make optimistic assumptions that are not sound.

There is no putting off to a more convenient season. "Watch unto prayer" is a rather unusual ordering of the words. We have heard, "Pray and watch." Peter was somewhat more specific when he wrote, "Watch unto prayer." Keep an eye on things and see where the need is. Servants, what do you actually face? Is it a matter of whether or not you will obey your master? Peter urged you are to do it. You may not feel like doing it. You need prayer; not to change things but to give you more strength. Wives are to be subject to their husbands. If husbands are sarcastic or demanding, wives will feel like talking up. Peter urged them to be quiet; they need prayer. Watch unto prayer. Husbands were told to treat their wives with respect, regardless. If any cannot do it, he needs prayer, from which will come strength that he needs. All believers with reference to each other are to be courteous with one another. If some with whom the believer has dealings are impossible, so that he cannot get along with them, the believer needs prayer. Watching unto prayer is practical and important.

BELIEVERS HAVE CHARITY TO OTHERS
(1 Peter 4:8-9)

Has anyone ever done something for you in such a half-hearted manner you wished he had not done anything at all?

> And above all things have fervent charity among yourselves: for charity shall cover the multitude of sins. Use hospitality one to another without grudging (1 Peter 4:8-9).

In this passage Peter gave practical guidance. Charity shall cover a multitude of sins. "Use hospitality one to another without grudging." These are important words. If Peter had used one text throughout this entire epistle it would have been, "Abstain from fleshly lusts." There may be no intrinsic evil in what the believer is doing, but if he does it to excess, Peter would warn him to abstain from his fleshly desires that war against his soul. This is not so much because any practice is evil but because the believer may not have time or strength for the good. We kill the weeds in the garden, not because they are evil, but for the sake of the vegetables. If this principle is true for vegetables in the garden, it is true for the soul.

If a believer is doing things to excess, and he plans to resign from the daily rounds, he will have to do some judging. To judge will require careful thought. The believer may realize that his business cannot afford for him to spend several afternoons a week playing golf. Hours spent on trivialities are not worth it. When the believer exercises judgment, the first thing he knows he will start judging other people. When one is critical of self, he starts being critical of others. This will pose a problem: in his efforts to do good, the believer finds fault with others. To offset this Peter wrote, "Above all things have fervent charity among yourselves." Far more important than any other consideration, the believer should be kind. This cannot be given too much consideration, too much emphasis, "for charity shall cover the multitude of sins." In dealing with fellow believers, first of all in his heart the believer should be kind. That is not really as hard as one would think.

For years I thought that phrase, "For charity shall cover a multitude of sins," meant that if I were charitable to others, it would cover a multitude of my sins; and the Lord would be gracious to me. In the course of Bible study it has become increasingly clear what that really means. Think back on a time when real charity was shown. When Noah was lying in his tent naked, Ham came and looked at him. Ham then went out and told about it. The other two sons, Shem and Japheth, took a garment and walking in backward covered their father, refusing even to look upon his nakedness. They covered his embarrassment, that which would have left Noah at a disadvantage. God saw this and blessed them. Noah also blessed them. This was very pleasing to God.

What is this saying to us? If I have charity toward any particular believer I will cover his sins, regardless of how many there are. What Ham did brought a curse from God. This means in a practical way I should never repeat anything that hurts someone else. God does not want me to do that. I should keep it to myself, that I might have the blessing of God.

BELIEVERS MINISTER TO EACH OTHER
(1 Peter 4:10-11)

Have you ever thought that when spiritual help is given, when one Christian helps another, this would be done as God's representative?

> As every man hath received the gift, even so minister the same one to another, as good stewards of the manifold grace of God. If any man speak, let him speak as the oracles of God; if any man minister, let him do it as of the ability which God giveth: that God in all things may be glorified through Jesus Christ, to whom be praise and dominion for ever and ever. Amen (1 Peter 4:10-11).

It would appear that certain members of the Body are given special grace, and this enables them to help other believers in a special way. This truth is to be found in various places in the Bible, and it is found particularly in the writings of Paul. In First Corinthians 12:8-11 we see that Paul said something about the gifts of the Spirit. There are diversities of gifts, differences of administration, but the same Lord.

> But the manifestation of the Spirit is given to every man to profit withal (1 Cor. 12:7).

Everybody can profit by it. There follows a list of those gifts.

> But all these worketh that one and the selfsame Spirit, dividing to every man severally as he will (1 Cor. 12:11).

Peter urged an important admonition upon all who have these special gifts. If a believer has a certain gift, if one has been given the ability to understand the meaning of a passage of Scripture, he can help others to grasp the meaning. It may be that in a given situation a number of people are faced with a problem, and one person has the ability to pray about the matter. Those who can interpret the Bible are to share this with people. They are to minister to one another as good stewards of the manifold grace of God. This grace is never their own, it belongs to God, and it is for them to use. "If any man speak, let him speak as the oracles of God; if any man minister, let him do it as of the ability which God giveth." Some will speak and some will preach, and they are supposed to do it as if God were speaking and preaching through them. Some people can take care of the sick, others can give money. Some can help with the building, and some can take care of the grounds. If a believer does minister, let him do it as of the ability that God giveth. It is truly "Christ in you" that enables the believer to see the meaning of that passage of Scripture. Let us always remember that all members have some gift, and all service is to be done that God may be glorified. The gift is "Christ in you" and there is no room for personal prestige; no credit to self.

SUFFERING IN ORDER TO REIGN
(1 Peter 4:12-13)

Have you realized that suffering is sure to come in the life of any believer in Christ?

> Beloved, think it not strange concerning the fiery trial which is to try you, as though some strange thing happened unto you: but rejoice, inasmuch as ye are partakers of Christ's sufferings; that, when his glory shall be revealed, ye may be glad also with exceeding joy (1 Peter 4:12-13).

In studying First Peter we should remember that suffering is a possibility for all believers at all times. Suffering is in the picture for all believers in Jesus Christ. Picture the happy smile of a five-year-old child when those front teeth are gone. Was there an accident—did someone knock those teeth out? No, that is part of the growing up process, and it is like this with the believer in Christ. Suffering is part of the normal experience of a child of God. The suffering of a believer is not exactly like the baking of an apple when placed in a hot oven. After baking, it is sweeter than it was before. Of course, it is true that if a believer in Christ has real trouble, he will emerge a better person. But this suffering has to do with the death of the ego. It is not a matter of just being humble; it is denying self unto death. There may be an emotional experience, and feelings may be hurt, but not necessarily so.

This suffering may be voluntary on the part of the believer. He may be willing to deny himself, and that would be suffering. But it may be forced upon him. Someone else may deny the believer, and he will have a similar experience. He will suffer in the flesh. He will die as a human being in order that he may live as a child of God. The language Peter used in these verses indicated that it could be a shock to a believer to have this happen. Peter recognized the affect this could have. For instance, when preparing to plant a garden, a neighbor might point out that the soil is such the finest vegetables will grow. What probably was left unsaid was that the soil would also grow the best weeds in the county; and if not properly fertilized a good crop would not ensue. Also, in that neighborhood big dogs were allowed to roam, making it necessary to put up a strong fence. Much about that garden might not be mentioned when the gardener was told it would grow the best vegetables in the county.

So it is with being a believer in Christ. Someone may say that if a person believes in the Lord Jesus Christ, he will be blessed. But did that person also point out that believing in the Lord Jesus Christ would mean that the believer must "deny" himself so that he may be blessed? It is true that when you are a believer in Christ you will be a happy man, because you will have the favor of God. But do you understand that being a believer in Christ means you must deny self, that you must suffer death, that you must give in and give up? Then you will be blessed.

In trying to prepare them for this, Peter wrote, "Think it not strange." The believer should not be upset, or think he is on the wrong road, because he is having trouble. He has committed himself to the Lord, and suddenly his neighbor is unpleasant, and at the office others are beginning to criticize him. He is running into all kinds of opposition. He may not understand why this is happening, since before he was a believer nothing went wrong. "Concerning the fiery trial which is to try you." Earlier Peter spoke about the faith which is more precious than gold though it be tried with fire. Fire is often spoken of as the means of testing faith. It is a case of testing confidence in the promises of God.

The believer should not think it strange that he is tested with fire as in persecution and suffering, as if some strange thing has happened. It may seem to be something that should not have happened at all. The believer can rejoice in the midst of this.

He can recall again and again the future promises. If he has lost his baby teeth he will get real teeth. That is the idea. When those weeds were growing in the garden, you hoed them out, and you got real tomatoes. The believer can have joy about this whole matter. He can keep on thinking about it and rejoice inasmuch as he is a partaker of Christ's suffering. The believer can keep in mind that if he suffers unto death he will reign unto life. The believer can yield himself to God, and God will take care of him.

Christ Jesus suffered. The climax of His life occurred as He went to the cross. He knew He was going there, but when He considered the glory that was coming afterward, when He remembered the promises, He endured the cross, despising the shame. And He sat down at the right hand of God. The glory of Christ is that although He suffered unto death, He was raised unto life. Although He yielded Himself as a lamb before his shearers is dumb, He was made the King of Kings and Lord of all. It was to the glory of the Lord Jesus Christ that He won out; and as He was victorious, so the believer will be. As a believer in Christ, if you are suffering, put yourself in the Lord's hands and rejoice. Just as it can be shown that Christ Jesus accomplished everything by suffering unto death, so that He should now be with the Father, so it can be shown that as the believer yields himself in suffering, he shall reign with Christ.

SHARING CHRIST'S REPROACH
(1 Peter 4:14-15)

Can you believe that anybody will be mistreated simply because he is a believer in Christ? Do you think anyone would object if you suggested prayer and Bible reading?

If ye be reproached for the name of Christ, happy are ye; for the spirit of glory and of God resteth upon you: on their part he is evil spoken of, but on your part he is glorified. But let none of you suffer as a murderer, or as a thief, or as an evildoer, or as a busybody in other men's matters (1 Peter 4:14-15).

In recent years opposition to any positive act or attitude of faith, such as praying or reading the Bible, has been pronounced in public. Public objection to the use of the name of Christ is widespread. There are places in our country today where a Christmas program in a public school is ruled out because the name of Christ would be used. Peter anticipated something like this, perhaps, and certainly the Holy Spirit knew we would need reassurance. We cannot be members of Christ's body without experiencing reproach. Peter referred to this opposition but offered no rebuttal. He did not say we should argue or fight, or insist on our rights. If someone mistreats a believer because he uses the name of Christ, that believer can be happy; he is sharing with the Lord Jesus Christ Himself. "On their part he is evil spoken of, but on your part he is glorified." You are for Him. Let it be that way.

There are ministers of the Gospel today who object to emphasis in public on public praying. Some will preach an entire sermon and never mention the Lord Jesus Christ as if He were a person. This is a serious failing. We should not miss the guidance from Peter in verse 14. Believers can recognize the opposition, they can be sorry that anyone should be that way, but they can rejoice to think that they are being classed with Christ.

However, Peter issues a warning: "Let none of you suffer as a murderer, or as a thief, or as an evildoer, or as a busybody in other men's matters." The Scripture tells us, "Whosoever hateth his brother is a murderer" (1 John 3:15). "As a thief": am I trying to get something for nothing? Something that does not belong to me? "As an evildoer": am I doing anything that is contrary to the Gospel? "Or as a busybody in other men's matters": am I intruding myself into the affairs of other people? Peter warns me that for suffering of that nature there is no relief.

CONFIDENCE IN CHRIST
(1 Peter 4:16-17)

Do you realize that a believer in Christ must expect to be criticized more often and more sharply than anybody else?

> Yet if any man suffer as a Christian, let him not be ashamed; but let him glorify God on this behalf. For the time is come that judgment must begin at the house of God: and if it first begin at us, what shall the end be of them that obey not the gospel of God? (1 Peter 4:16-17).

When a man lets it be known in public that he believes in the Lord Jesus Christ, he suffers because he dared to openly affirm his faith and to be received into the membership of the church. The public readily criticizes the church. When the Gospel is criticized we wonder how that can be, because it is good news of God's love and mercy toward men, trying to get people to turn to God. A community readily criticizes the preacher, almost everything about him. This often includes Sunday school teachers and choir members. It almost seems as though people actually derive malicious pleasure in finding fault with anything that has to do with the church. We do not always recognize the inspiration of this ill-will. The natural man feels that he is indicted because of his sin; he feels he is on the defensive, and in self-defense he will seek to find fault with others. Some will seek to find fault with God, and these are usually critical of anyone who says he is a believer in Christ.

Suppose a man has lived in a community for some years, and has made no profession of faith. Let us say he is addicted to drink. Now let this man become a believer in Christ. He will immediately attract all kinds of opposition and criticism. Peter would say, "Let him not be ashamed." The word "ashamed" here means not so much that he should be embarrassed but that he should not stumble, or become upset about this. "But let him glorify God on this behalf." This glorifying God means that he would praise God, remembering that God is on his side. Furthermore, he would be glorifying God if, by putting his trust in the Lord, he quietly endured what ill-will was shown. When accused falsely and ridiculed, he would be meek and humble and accept the criticism. This would be glorifying God.

"For the time is come that judgment must begin at the house

of God: and if it first begin at us, what shall the end be of them that obey not the gospel of God?" The believer in Christ may suffer just because he is a believer. Some may wonder what kind of suffering that would be. It might be that when he joins the church he will find that some people will be unfair to him, or discourteous. Before, they were friendly; now they will have nothing to do with him. There will be all sorts of rumors. He may be omitted from any kind of honorable mention, no matter how much good he does. If this should be the case, let that believer in Christ rejoice. He can accept this treatment as evidence that he belongs to the Lord Jesus Christ; for that is the way He was treated. Being humble and meek is part of the victory. If the member of Christ's body believes God will take care of him it makes no difference what men may do. The very fact that the believer is already reconciled to God delivers him from any accusations which may come. The believer in Christ already has everything taken care of between him and God, and no one can harm him when he trusts in the Lord.

THE TRUSTING CONDUCT OF THE BELIEVER
(1 Peter 4:18-19)

Do you have any idea what a believer in Christ can do to endure suffering?

> And if the righteous scarcely be saved, where shall the ungodly and the sinner appear? Wherefore let them that suffer according to the will of God commit the keeping of their souls to him in well doing, as unto a faithful Creator (1 Peter 4:18-19).

This entire epistle of Peter is really, in a sense, a private matter. Peter was writing to believers who were strangers in this world. The suffering of a believer in Christ who has to endure self-denial and misery is very painful. Although unkind things may be said about believers in Christ they try to show a cheerful and gracious attitude in return. "And if the righteous scarcely be saved, where shall the ungodly and the sinner appear?" We need make no mistake; one day there will be judgment upon all. "Let them that suffer according to the will of God." The believer in Christ may have suffered when he did not deserve it; he was not causing it, but God allowed it to come to him. He should be one of those who "commit the keeping of their souls to him in well doing."

The believer worships God in public and in private. The day should not start or end without worshiping Him. The believer will go to church, will read his Bible, and will practice prayer. He will turn to God, and seek His face. He will have rules to follow and regulations to obey; he will keep them, do them, obey them. This is doing good. The believer will keep in mind that God made him and God watches over him. He will trust Him. God has taken care of him. So, as unto a faithful Creator, the believer will commit the keeping of his soul to God in well doing.

FIRST PETER
Chapter 5

✝ ✝ ✝

THE DUTY OF ELDERS
(1 Peter 5:1-4)

Why should a believer in Christ take responsibility for the spiritual welfare of anyone else?

> The elders which are among you I exhort, who am also an elder, and a witness of the sufferings of Christ, and also a partaker of the glory that shall be revealed: Feed the flock of God which is among you, taking the oversight thereof, not by constraint, but willingly; not for filthy lucre, but of a ready mind; neither as being lords over God's heritage, but being examples to the flock (1 Peter 5:1-3).

The natural person is inclined to think on any given day that it is his business to look after only himself. Since he thinks no one else will do this, he feels justified. That is not the way Jesus of Nazareth lived. It is natural but it is not spiritual. Christ came into this world for the express purpose of doing for others, and if you have Christ in you, that is the way it will work out in you. While this could be true of all believers in Christ, Peter makes a point in these verses of showing what the example of an elder should be. The elder will constantly seek to help others, not so much because others are deserving, nor because God will make them worth it, but because God cares about them.

"Elder" is a word given to those who would be called leaders. If you think in terms of a tribe, he would be the chieftain; if you think in terms of a company of soldiers, he would be the captain; and if you think in terms of a football team, he would be the coach. The elders, then, are those who lead other people because they have had experience, and they know more about Christ than the average person. Peter has something to say to them since he was one of them himself. Peter had been an eyewitness of the death of the Lord Jesus Christ on Calvary. He was the "partaker of the glory which shall be revealed" because he had the experience of being born again and of being raised, as it were, from the dead and entering into the fullness of life. He was present on the day of Pentecost when Almighty God came to dwell in their hearts, and promised that in the future they would be with Him. What he knew about Christ and could show to others gave him this responsibility of leadership.

Peter wrote to the elders, "Feed the flock of God which is among you." The Lord is their Shepherd, and they are His sheep. Someone has pointed out that it is not a case of shearing them and selling the wool; the elders were to feed the flock of God, bringing them the truth of God. They were to make sure the flock understood the things of the Gospel. "Taking the oversight thereof, not by constraint, but willingly." The elders were to assume responsibility of leading others, not because they had to do this, but because they wanted to do this. "Not for filthy lucre, but of a ready mind." Filthy lucre refers to money. Many think this means that money is bad. "Lucre" refers to silver and when you say "filthy lucre" some infer it is all bad; however, only that money that is received for the wrong reason is bad. "But of a ready mind." This is why they are to do it. "Neither as being lords over God's heritage, but being examples to the flock."

> And when the chief Shepherd shall appear, ye shall receive a crown of glory that fadeth not away (1 Peter 5:4).

Sometimes when a person has taught Sunday school or is an officer in the church, he is tempted to feel and act overbearing. Peter warned against this. Paul said that the Thessalonian believers were his crown for rejoicing. A parent can feel that way about children brought to the Lord, and a pastor can feel that way about his members.

HUMILITY IS THE KEY
(1 Peter 5:5)

Have you ever thought how simple it is to win the favor of God?

> Likewise, ye younger, submit yourselves unto the elder. Yea, all of you be subject one to another, and be clothed with humility: for God resisteth the proud, and giveth grace to the humble (1 Peter 5:5).

In this verse we see the plan of God to bless us. We are to submit ourselves unto those who are over us and be subject one to another. We are to be humble. God resisteth the proud, but He giveth grace to the humble. God has arranged that we do not live alone and He deals with us according to the way in which we live. We are to follow Peter's admonition as we have it set forth before us here. "Ye younger" is not just a matter of being young in years. One can be younger in experience or in ability. This term refers to those who have not had the fullest experience or who are dependent upon other people.

The elders have already been told what to do, and now the younger ones are to do the way the elders do. The younger people are to be humble in their obedience. They are to follow this principle for blessing: submit themselves; accept the rules as they are. Probably all regulations work a hardship on some. What should be done? The faithful believer should yield humbly. Those who selfishly and arrogantly take the license to do as they please will not have the blessing of God. Peter would say to them, "Yield to the rules and regulations." The young should submit to the elders. This is emphasized here.

The New Testament teaches that we are to submit ourselves. Submission is simple; one needs just to give in. But it is to be total, and we are to submit in everything. The real wisdom in this is not the wisdom of those in control, but rather the obedience of the person being controlled. Those who submit want the favor of God, and they that are humble enough to do that will receive the blessing. "Yea, all of you be subject one to another, and be clothed with humility." This includes everyone. The wife will be submissive to the husband, but he will be thoughtful of the wife; children will obey their parents, but parents will care for the children. Believers in Christ will all be considerate of each other. "For God resisteth the proud, and giveth grace to the humble." What a simple yet profound statement! He will enable you to follow these precepts and comfort you as you do.

GOD'S CARE FOR THE BELIEVER
(1 Peter 5:6-7)

Did you know that no believer in Christ ever need bear his burden alone?

> Humble yourselves therefore under the mighty hand of God,
> that he may exalt you in due time: casting all your care upon him;
> for he careth for you (1 Peter 5:6-7).

This is probably the most wonderful promise offered to struggling human beings. A believer in Christ has human strength and understanding just as others have; yet he is just as weak and limited and patchy as that sounds. But he can trust in God and receive help. For many people, life is a battle; a discouraging series of defeats. They try and they are defeated. It is common to feel defeat in our very bones and thus to experience frustration. Perhaps some of it is our own fault, but it is still real. Our wishes may be too ambitious; our goals may be too high. Our procedures may be unwise; we may long for things we cannot have.

The Bible does not deny we will have trouble; that we will struggle and lose. "In the world ye shall have tribulation" (John 16:33). But Peter wrote: "Humble yourselves therefore under the mighty hand of God." How can a believer do this? Will he accept the idea that the mighty hand of God is over him? If so, he is exactly where God wants him to be. If the believer is a housewife, that is her life; she may be a secretary, in that case she should accept her situation. Tomorrow it may be different; but right now she will humble herself and accept herself for what she is. Remember, God can make changes, "that he may exalt you in due time." This seems to be God's way. Joseph first served in prison, and finally served at the head of the government. Moses first served as a shepherd, and later he became the great liberator of his people. Gideon served on his father's farm and did his work in hiding for fear of the Midianites, but God called him and placed him in charge of the nation. David was a fugitive, running from pillar to post, trying to escape being killed by Saul, but he later became king. The believer should not complain about his lot in life. He should accept it, whatever it may be. God can give him grace, and God will watch over him.

"Casting all your care upon him." The believer will have cares, so he should not ignore them. He should take his cares to God; he should not neglect them.

OUR ADVERSARY THE DEVIL
(1 Peter 5:8-9)

Are you conscious of the fact that the danger of being ensnared by the devil is always present? Do you think the devil is real?

> Be sober, be vigilant; because your adversary the devil, as a roaring lion, walketh about, seeking whom he may devour: whom resist stedfast in the faith, knowing that the same afflictions are accomplished in your brethren that are in the world (1 Peter 5:8-9).

There is much in the spiritual world we do not know, but we are sure in our conviction there is a God. Although we have never seen Him; God is. We would never have known Him if He had not revealed Himself to us. Is heaven real? Is hell real? And is the Holy Spirit real? Those who deny that these are real remind me of the blind man saying that no rose is red, having never seen one.

The Lord Jesus was the Son of God, and He was incarnate in this world, living as the Son of Man. He told things that were true; and He could be depended upon. A man once asked if I believed in heaven. I answered, "Yes, because Jesus Christ did." When he asked if I believed there is a devil, and hell, and I answered in the affirmative, he said, "It seems to me that everything you say depends on one person, on Jesus Christ." He added that I made him think about a man who is hanging by one nail on the wall, and if that nail were to give way, if Jesus Christ were not true, where would I be? I told him I would be sunk. Then I added, "But suppose that nail does not give way; suppose Jesus Christ actually is true: then where will I be?" And he said, "I suppose you would say you would be saved." And that is what I do depend upon. In closing the conversation I did ask the young man what nail he was hanging on.

Peter urged sobriety and vigilance in view of this danger. Satan is active; he is right now prowling around to see whom he can destroy. There should be no collaboration with him. How can one resist Satan? I can offer several suggestions: first, read your Bible. Satan does not want you to do this. If he has his way you will always have something else to do. In the matter of prayer, the devil does not want you to pray. "The devil trembles when he sees the weakest saint upon his knees." Whenever a Christian prays in the name of the Lord Jesus Christ, he is as safe as he possibly can be, insofar as Satan is concerned. The devil does not want you to go to church, but if you go you will be resisting him. He wants you to criticize the preacher, and he will want you to find fault with the people, and with the choir and the choir director. If you do not, you will be resisting him.

When it comes to dealing with people, the devil would have you take offense. The devil wants you to be selfish. If you give to the poor, if you are kind to people and help them, that is not what the devil wants. Resist the devil. Turn yourself over to God. Then you can have in mind that all this is not new; others have done it. "The same afflictions are accomplished in your brethren that are in the world." It is not unusual that you should have to resist Satan, so do not be naive. Remember that the devil is like a roaring lion, seeking whom he may devour. So stay close to the Lord Jesus Christ.

THE ETERNAL GLORY OF GOD
(1 Peter 5:10-11)

Do you realize God works in the believer to make him mature?

> But the God of all grace, who hath called us unto his eternal glory by Christ Jesus, after ye have suffered a while, make you perfect, stablish, strengthen, settle you. To him be glory and dominion for ever and ever. Amen (1 Peter 5:10-11).

Everything that is ever done for the believer is the work of God. We readily confess that no man is able; his help comes from God, who is gracious. No part of salvation is earned by man; it is received from the Lord Jesus Christ. God is "the God of all grace, who hath called us unto his eternal glory by Christ Jesus." What is meant by His eternal glory? The word "glory" refers to the fulfillment of a potential, like harvest time. The glory of God appears when He gets the job done, and His eternal glory is when He gets the job done for all eternity. Now the glory of God throughout eternity will be what He does through His Son. What is revealed to us through the Word of God, then, is that the Father gets things done through the Son. What did He undertake to do that would glorify Him? Was it not that He would produce brethren like unto the Lord Jesus Christ? His Son was to be the first-born among many brethren. He created man in His own image. Man was to have had fellowship with Him. He gave His Son a body like unto these creatures He had created; so that His Son might be the first-born among many brethren. These creatures, human beings, would actually be like the Lord Jesus Christ.

When God made Adam in the image of God this was not yet good enough. Adam was made in the flesh, and flesh and blood could not inherit the kingdom. What Adam never could do, Christ Jesus actually did. Children of Adam who are believers in Christ are something more than Adam ever was. Adam was made of the flesh, but believers in Christ are made by the grace of God in Christ Jesus. In this way God received His children by having them be born again. Each believer was made once as a child of Adam, then born again as a child of God. The purpose of God was to produce brethren like unto Him, and this He accomplished through Christ Jesus. He had Christ Jesus come into this world made in fashion as a man, actually taking on Him the nature of Adam that in it He might die and be resurrected. So the way was opened for children of Adam through faith to become brethren of Jesus, the only begotten Son.

This is the procedure by which God accomplishes His work. He has the flesh die and then He has the individual raised from the dead by the power of God because of faith in Jesus Christ. As Jesus Christ was raised from the dead so will be those who have fallen asleep in Him. This the language implies.

Here we have this word "suffering" again. "But the God of all grace, who hath called us unto his eternal glory by Christ Jesus, after ye have suffered a while, make you perfect." Remember, the word "suffer" means "dying in the flesh"—"after you have been dying in the flesh for awhile." Apparently, dying in the flesh is not instantaneous. Maybe it is not a uniform process, and maybe it does not take the same time for everybody. Some grow fast, some grow slowly. Some die fast, some die slowly. When we say, "Dying in the flesh for a while," it does not mean that you have to experience suffering and being in misery and then, as a kind of reward, God relieves you from it and brings you on in. You must be born again and then He will make you perfect, bringing you to maturity. You will be wholly yielded, totally set apart and sanctified unto God so that you can truthfully say, "None of self, but all of Thee."

In verse 10 we find the closing words, "Stablish, strengthen, and settle you." "Stablish"—make you so you will not be shaken; "strengthen"—make you strong. Peter's prayer was that God, who hath called us unto His eternal glory, after we have suffered for awhile; after having experienced self-denial unto death, will make us whole.

THE TRUE GRACE OF GOD
(1 Peter 5:12-14)

Has it ever occurred to you that people may have wrong ideas about the grace of God as it is received by believers?

By Silvanus, a faithful brother unto you, as I suppose, I have written briefly, exhorting, and testifying that this is the true grace of God wherein ye stand. The church that is at Babylon, elected together with you, saluteth you; and so doth Marcus my son. Greet ye one another with a kiss of charity. Peace be with you all that are in Christ Jesus. Amen (1 Peter 5:12-14).

With these verses Peter concludes his epistle, which was sent by Silvanus (thought to be the same as Silas). Peter seems to have feared that people might get the wrong idea of the grace of God. In writing this first epistle, he is apparently undertaking to explain to believers in Christ what it really means to receive the grace of God. It would be easy for some to think that God in grace would let just anyone come. This would be an error; God will accept only those who are in Christ Jesus. "This is my beloved Son in whom I am well pleased." Then again, it may have been supposed that this matter of getting right with God would be an achievement that would be possible for people who were good, or strong. This would also be an error. God will accept no man on his works; salvation is a free gift. Now it will be a gift and it will be free but only those who take it will get it, regardless of what they have done within themselves. There is only one way to the grace of God; it is the way of the cross that leads home.

We read, "This is the true grace of God wherein ye stand." This is the key to the whole book. When he says the "true" grace of God, he implies there could have been other ideas but this is the truth about suffering and glory: the cross, Calvary; and then the resurrection and the crown. In discussing suffering Peter always meant suffering unto death because this is the only way there can be newness of life. Doubtless there are people who have the idea that this suffering is a kind of probationary period, as if a reward could be earned through suffering. That is not true. The suffering is not complete until you give yourself up entirely to God. It is after you have given yourself to God that you will suffer in the death of yourself.

In sending his epistle by Silvanus, Peter speaks of him as a "faithful brother unto you, as I suppose." When he says "I suppose" he is not doubting it at all. It is a way of saying Silvanus is a faithful brother according to my book. "I have written briefly" (concisely). Time and time again Peter spoke plainly and to the point. He did not speak of his own experiences; he simply stated it as it was. "Exhorting" (calling upon everyone to take this seriously; Peter wanted his people to realize that the way into blessing is the way of the cross; it is the way of suffering). "And testifying that this is the true grace of God wherein ye stand" (telling the world that this is the real truth, reminding men that this was the basis for their faith).

Verse 13 may seem rather strange, "The church that is at Babylon, elected together with you, saluteth you; and so doth Marcus my son." This could be paraphrased to read, "Those that are at Babylon, elected together with you, salute you and so does Marcus, my son." The word "elect" is not select, not chosen in a sense there are only a few favorites. He is saying the people at Babylon, who are called together with these other Christians, salute you. Salute in the way a sailor from one part of a boat would wave at another member of the crew, in mutual fellowship, greeting one another like fellow travelers in the same caravan, or fellow soldiers in the same army. "Greet ye one another with a kiss of charity." We must consider the customs of the day. A good translation of that is sometimes found in the newer versions, as, "Greet each other with a symbol of goodwill, of kindness toward each other." "Peace be with you all that are in Christ Jesus."

All of the gracious promises of God are true only for those who are in Christ Jesus. God deals with all men; He is the God of all the earth. Every single human being will stand before Him, whether he is a believer in Christ or not. There are some special folks, who are special in that they have received Jesus Christ as their Savior. This is the way of truth. This is not world-wide peace, peace for everybody. There can be peace only for those who are in Christ Jesus. This sweeping grace is definitely limited to those who are in Christ Jesus. And so, we have come to the end of the first epistle of Peter. We have found this apostle earnestly speaking to believing souls, showing them the grace of God which is in Christ Jesus.

SECOND PETER
Chapter 1

† † †

PETER WROTE TO FELLOW-BELIEVERS
(2 Peter 1:1-2)

Have you realized that the benefits of the Gospel of Christ are given to believers, who have the knowledge of God?

> Simon Peter, a servant and an apostle of Jesus Christ, to them that have obtained like precious faith with us through the righteousness of God and our Saviour Jesus Christ: Grace and peace be multiplied unto you through the knowledge of God, and of Jesus our Lord (2 Peter 1:1-2).

These are the first two verses in the book of Second Peter. Notice here how we have Simon Peter himself referred to, using his two names. Simon was the name he had in his early life, "Men call thee Simon," and Peter is the name given to him by the Lord Jesus Christ, "Thou shalt be called Peter." He was a man among men and a child of God, a man whom men knew as a fisherman and a servant with whom the Lord dealt. "A servant and an apostle of Jesus Christ." The word "servant" refers to his personal relationship with the Lord, in which Peter counts the Lord as Master and is committed to Him, to obey Him in everything. "And an apostle" means that Peter was somebody entrusted with a message. Peter was a servant in his relation to the Lord and an apostle in his relation towards the world. He had an authoritative message he was to give to the world.

This man, Simon Peter, had a message "to them that have obtained like precious faith with us." This is speaking to them not as if they were superior people with remarkable records. He does not say a thing about their records, or about their works. The distinctive characteristics of these people to whom he was writing was this: they were the fortunate recipients of the grace of God. Being a believer in Christ is not a matter of being something by one's own works or one's own conduct; it is being something by the grace of God. The grace of God is set forth in the promises of Scripture, and received as any soul responds by believing in God.

A recent translation of the New Testament puts this sentence this way: "To those who through the righteousness of our God and Saviour, Jesus Christ, have been given a faith as precious as ours, may grace and peace be yours in full measure through your knowledge of God and of Jesus our Lord."

Everything believers have in the Gospel began with Jesus of Nazareth. His righteousness was His willing and competent service to God His Father, in which He died for us. What He did in His service made available to us His righteousness on the basis of our obedience to Him.

When the sinner receives the Gospel of Jesus Christ he is given the inner disposition to trust God. With his knowledge of God and Christ Jesus, the Lord, the believer can receive the promises that involve grace and peace. Believers are given a faith as precious as Peter's. Peter went on to pray: "May grace and peace be multiplied unto you." The fullness of blessing will be overflowing through the knowledge of God and Jesus Christ our Lord. This grace is an inward enablement to obey God, to respond to His Word. Peace is the inward experience of rest.

How will the knowledge of God bring this grace and peace? The believer believes the promises when he knows God. These promises involve grace and peace. If the believer in Christ has the knowledge of God and of Jesus Christ our Lord, he will know that God sent Jesus Christ into the world to seek and to save the lost. If he knows that God sent Jesus Christ into the world to seek and to save the lost, and he realizes that he personally is a lost person, it will come to him that if he believes in Jesus Christ he will be saved. In that way he is being led into the grace of God.

There are other ways in which this can be done. In the knowledge of God, the believer can have in mind that God is all powerful and almighty and that He can be trusted. If the believer will act accordingly, he can in faith, by putting his knowledge of God to the test, put his whole trust in God. Thus he will receive the peace of God that passeth all understanding. The more any person believes, the more he receives. And what he receives will be grace and peace through the knowledge of God. We are reminded of what Paul wrote to Titus, "Not by works of righteousness which we have done, but according to his mercy he saved us" (Titus 3:5).

THE MESSAGE OF SECOND PETER
(2 Peter summary)

Do you realize that after any work or project is begun there is much to be learned that was unexpected?

A man will often spend more time thinking about whether he should buy a car than he will spend in studying about its care after he has it. Is it not also true that young people often spend far more time in courtship trying to persuade each other they should belong together than they spend in planning a home where they will live together? Oftentimes a person is more concerned about getting a job than he is about doing the job. This is also true in spiritual matters. People spend time thinking, studying, and wondering before they become believers, while they spend little time afterwards thinking about how to live as a believer.

It is almost as though a young couple is supposed to think that after they have the wedding ceremony it is all over and there is nothing more to learn. Can anything be more naive? Actually, the time spent before is relatively unimportant because you had not really invested yourself. But afterwards you are "in it"; you belong to it. You may take a long time to decide if you will get into the boat, but afterwards you are interested in where the boat is going.

Now in the New Testament this is seen in a number of cases where we have second letters. In First Corinthians the Apostle Paul discusses the problems of conduct in that church; then in Second Corinthians he discusses the normal pattern without the problems. The second epistle set out more clearly what the first epistle dealt with; and also gives warning. In First Thessalonians the general emphasis is the return of the Lord, which is mentioned at the close of each of the five chapters. In Second Thessalonians we have the authentic pattern of the return of the Lord, a warning of how the return of the Lord can be misunderstood and misapplied.

In First Timothy he tells ways of right witnessing, while in Second Timothy he gives a picture of what it means to be a good soldier. This second epistle also gave a warning: how easily one can be misled. With reference to the epistles of John: we have First John in which the apostle wrote about fellowship in the Lord, while in Second John a few words point out the new commandment that we love one another, as well as the warning about taking folks into fellowship who should not be there. The first epistle of Peter sets forth the true grace of God, and Second Peter describes how the true grace of God is operative. There is also a stern warning about those who would mislead. First Peter ends with the statement, "I have written briefly, exhorting, and testifying that this is the true grace of God wherein ye stand." This epistle gives instruction as to how a believer can cultivate this grace of God in him. The more he understands it, the better it will be for him. This invites the believer to listen. But at once there is a warning about men who preach and teach of the grace of God in a way that leads into barrenness. Here is another warning against error. Sometimes evangelical Christians can tell what is in the Gospel, but show in their lives a woeful lack of evidence that they themselves obey the Gospel.

The Gospel of the Lord Jesus Christ comes to man in the form of an invitation, but he must understand the invitation for it to become important. The hearer must come to Jesus for the invitation to be valid. The Gospel gives directives, but obviously, if a person does not obey, it will not be any good. So the preaching of the Gospel points where to go and implies that the hearer should go. Thus the preaching of the Gospel embodies the imperative, "Come unto me." The same is also true with the imperative "abide."

> Abide in me, and I in you. As the branch cannot bear fruit of itself, except it abide in the vine; no more can ye, except ye abide in me (John 15:4).

How can the words of God abide in a man? Through his study of the Scriptures. He needs to get the Bible into his bones. This is a directive. Again, there is the imperative "go." The Bible tells the disciples of Christ, "Go and teach them all things whatsoever I have commanded you." That will be valid only when they go.

The Gospel tells the truth about God and this should lead a man to worship. If a man understands the truth about God, he should bow down his heart to Him. This truth will lead a man to repent: he should freely confess before God that he is a sinner in God's sight. This would be repentance. The truth about God and His mercy and grace should lead a person to repent and believe. The Bible also tells the truth about man and that should lead the hearer to respect man and to be considerate of others. The believer should have charity toward the poor. The Bible tells the truth about praying, and that leads to praying. If a person just hears about this truth and never does it, the truth will not do him any good. The Bible tells believers about the lost, and when the truth about the lost is known, believers are led to witnessing.

Second Peter emphasizes that believers should carry through and do what they are called to do, and warns them about being barren and unfruitful.

EXCEEDING GREAT PROMISES
(2 Peter 1:3-4)

Do you know how a person can escape the degeneration going on in this world?

> According as his divine power hath given unto us all things that pertain unto life and godliness, through the knowledge of him that hath called us to glory and virtue: whereby are given unto us exceeding great and precious promises: that by these ye might be partakers of the divine nature, having escaped the corruption that is in the world through lust (2 Peter 1:3-4).

The Gospel of Christ concerns us as we live in this world. It has elements that threaten to hurt and to destroy: accidents, calamity, famine, pestilence, war. About all of these, as believers in Christ, we must trust Providence. God is in control, which is shown in the fact that we often call these things acts of God. I also have elements in me that can hurt and destroy: foolishness, carelessness, laziness, sickness, death. In all of these things I would, as a believer in Christ, gladly trust that the grace of God in Christ Jesus can overcome; because where sin abounded grace does much more abound.

In these verses Peter refers to life and godliness. Believers have been given all things that pertain unto life and godliness. The word "life" is used over against death—life in place of death; living in place of dying; and godliness, the will of God, in place of the will of man. It means a person doing the work of God and the will of God in place of sinning. So Peter wrote of giving to us things that pertain unto life rather than unto death; unto godliness rather than unto sin. Notice again the words "glory" and "virtue," which believers have been called to share. Glory refers to the effectual operation of the grace of God in the heart of a person. Believers have been called to this relationship with God so that He will accomplish His purpose in them. As they bear much fruit, God is glorified. "Herein is my Father glorified, that ye bear much fruit." This fruit that they bear is the consequence of the life of God operating in them, and this brings about the glory.

The word "virtue" refers to the conduct that is visible: their life in the community, in their homes, and in this world. When a believer is inwardly led by the will of the Lord Jesus Christ, he will show outward results which the world will call virtue.

Let us notice some other phrases we have here. "According as his divine power . . ." Whenever we think of the divine power, and we have power in the New Testament, we can think of the resurrection of the Lord Jesus Christ; that is where power was demonstrated. This divine power does not come to us out of the blue sky; this divine power does not operate in us while we are lying in bed at night; this divine power works in the resurrection of the Lord Jesus Christ and then through Him in us if we believe in Him. "Hath given unto us all things," in the resurrection of the Lord Jesus Christ, all things are made available to us, and we believe all the problems of living are potentially solved. I need only enter into an understanding of what Christ Jesus did for me when He was raised from the dead to solve problems I will have.

The "exceeding great and precious promises" are those mentioned in verse 3 and also "through the knowledge of him that hath called us to glory and virtue." It is as I know God that I become acquainted with the promises which are given to me through the resurrection of the Lord Jesus Christ. I now have access to them, I can enter into them. "That by these ye might be partakers of the divine nature." This divine nature that is in Christ Jesus is what we can share in faith, by believing in Him as He was raised from the dead by the power of God. Committing ourselves to Christ is the way it all ties together. God speaks the promise to us, "Whosoever believeth in me shall not perish but have everlasting life."

"Having escaped the corruption that is in the world through lust," that is, having escaped by the resurrection. Now the corruption that is in the world through lust does not refer only to the corruption that is in other people's lives. No, it is the corruption that is active and operative in human nature, in everybody; the corruption with which lust, or selfish desire, has infected all mankind. It is the inevitable disintegration of the person that lust, or personal desire, produces in the whole world.

So we have in these verses a complete sketch of what the Gospel presents to each person. Salvation: this work of God in saving us is by the power of God according to the promises that are revealed to us in Christ Jesus unto all, whosoever will, to the glory of God. And this is what Peter is talking about.

ADDING TO FAITH
(2 Peter 1:5)

Do you realize that living the life of faith goes beyond accepting Christ?

> And beside this, giving all diligence, add to your faith virtue; and to virtue knowledge (2 Peter 1:5).

What does Peter mean when he says, "Beside this"? He means besides what he had said previously, in verses 3 and 4; beside believing in the crucifixion, the burial and the resurrection of Jesus Christ, and beside receiving from God in His promises the privilege of becoming a partaker of the divine nature. All of this is through faith, and this is the beginning. The life in Christ is begun thus: "If any man will come after me, let him deny himself, and take up his cross, and follow me" (Matt. 16:24).

In speaking of himself the apostle Paul could say, "I am crucified with Christ." This is the essential; other things come afterwards, beyond this. In your faith you believe in God and commit yourself to Him. Peter says, "Giving all diligence," that is, exercising every effort, applying yourself in dedicated commitment, being serious about it.

Let us look at the phrase, "add to your faith." You begin your relationship with Christ by believing, and believing leads into more. This is not a matter of bringing in something else, but of going on with what you have. If you think in terms of an apple tree growing, you first have the tree with the trunk and branches, and with bark on the trunk and leaves on the branches. Add to those, apple blossoms, then fruit. As flowers and fruit are added to an apple tree, so you are to continue in work, add to your faith, keep believing, until fruit begins to appear.

The first result that will appear is virtue. When we use the word "virtue" we mean what anybody would understand by the word: good conduct or good habits. This word "good" is not a passive word, implying that anything is good that is not bad. It is more than that. Good and bad are very much like light and dark; a person can say anything is light that is not dark, but that is too passive. You can say anything is dark that is not light, and that is true; and so you can say evil is there when good is not, and that is truer.

Good in itself implies something that is positive. So it is with light; the sun shines and it accomplishes things. Darkness is emptiness. When a person lives a good life it is good for himself and for others. What would really be good? One of the first things is reverence; no person is good who is not reverent. A person must honor and worship God. Next comes respect.

Respect those in authority over you. You will consider other people, when driving your car, for instance. And finally, charity will be shown to the poor, the disadvantaged. This adds up to virtue and will come to you if you are a believing person. You do not stand still and do nothing wrong to be good; but you really do something good. Whenever you see the word "good," put the little preposition "for" after it, and say "good for." And when you say someone is good, you mean he is good for something.

As you are a believing person, Christ Jesus, working in you, produces results. You will add to your virtue, knowledge. Knowledge of the natural world is part of science. What men have done and how they act is studied in social science. Learn the knowledge of living: how to live in the home, in business, in your country, and in the world. If you are a good person and you want to help others, you will try to understand everything you possibly can. The knowledge you acquire will be always within the perspective of Christ Jesus, and learning is the way it will come to you as you live in the Lord.

TEMPERANCE, PATIENCE, GODLINESS
(2 Peter 1:6)

Have you ever noticed that in order to be patient a person must have self-control?

> And to knowledge temperance; and to temperance patience; and to patience godliness (2 Peter 1:6).

The apostle is now urging these people to come closer in obedience to God, following faith through to certain results; they are to add a series of characteristics, one after another. The word "temperance" is commonly translated self-control, and best understood that way. In listing these characteristics Peter is not listing a number of equal things like petals on a blossom, or like cogs in a wheel. Peter speaks of this the way we have the expression in the Bible—first the blade, then the ear, then the full corn in the ear. There is significance in the succession of these traits. You need one to get to the next, and all of this begins with faith as brought out in verses 3 and 4: believing in Christ Jesus; getting the heart and soul oriented in the presence of God.

Now believing in Christ Jesus, getting the heart and soul oriented in the presence of God, putting your trust and confidence in Him, this produces virtue, which we noticed in our last study. And this virtue enables a person to learn honestly: he gets knowledge. It is when a person knows things that he is able to develop self-control and temperance. When a person establishes self-control it is possible to be what the Bible calls "patient." This is not so much patience when someone does something to hurt you; this patience is persistence, looking for results. James said that the husbandman, when he puts the grain in the ground, waiteth with long patience for the early and latter rain. He waits through the summer for the harvest, because in the providence of God things take time.

To this patience, or self-control, you will add godliness: a whole manner of life which is as God would have it be; in His presence, you are conscious of the things of God and have real trust in Him. It does not mean you will be as perfect as God is; it means that you will be conscious of Him; you will think about Him. I am not at all sure that godliness necessarily refers to the description of a certain type of perfection, such as is in virtue. Godliness is being conscious of God, looking toward and walking with Him. Christ Jesus lived this life in perfect godliness. He was always conscious of the presence of God. You can be always conscious of God if you are faithful and persistent in walking in the ways of God.

GODLINESS, BROTHERLY KINDNESS, CHARITY
(2 Peter 1:7)

Have you ever thought that if a person has brotherly kindness in his heart, he still needs to grow more to have charity also?

And to godliness brotherly kindness; and to brotherly kindness charity (2 Peter 1:7).

Second Peter is commonly quoted among Bible students as that Scripture which deals with the end of the world and with false prophets; yet it has much meaningful instruction about spiritual living, as we have seen in this first chapter. This may well be the principal idea in Second Peter, to encourage and to strengthen believers in their personal lives.

This study is focused upon the last of three verses which sketch the procedure to follow if one wants to grow in spiritual things. Peter listed in succession a series of traits or characteristics which can be cultivated to advantage by a Christian. We have read Peter's emphasis upon virtue, after which came knowledge and self-control, then patience and now godliness, brotherly kindness, and charity. These various characteristics are related to each other, and in this verse we read that we are to add to godliness brotherly kindness; and to brotherly kindness charity.

Remember, godliness does not show in the way one walks, or the clothes one wears. It is an inward consciousness, and it does not mean that I think I am as good as God or that I do what God does. It means, rather, that I am conscious of being in the presence of God. Because of this I act in a certain way and that becomes godly action. It is a relationship and attitude on my part toward the Father; when I look up to Him I remember that He gave His Son for me and that He is now watching over me. If I am in the presence of God, so are other believers; we all belong to one another, and thus I am interested in other believers. And if I am in the presence of God I have a certain attitude toward the whole world. I am a stranger and a pilgrim here; I am passing through.

If I am in the presence of God and am conscious of the things God has done, so that I can speak of myself as sharing in this experience of godliness, I will have a certain attitude toward myself, an attitude of self-denial. To godliness we are to add brotherly kindness. One would think that would follow automatically, but it doesn't. I need to believe. If I am conscious of the presence of God and enter into fellowship with Him, a certain attitude will develop: helpfulness to the people in my home, in my church, and in my neighborhood. Toward these people I will have a kind feeling. "And to brotherly kindness charity"—seeking the welfare and the happiness of others because they are creatures of God. The fact that they are persons for whom Christ died means that I am called by the grace of God to have an interest in their welfare.

I do not have to approve them. In our day there is a great deal made of a phrase, "acceptance as persons." This is not a matter of approving them as persons. There are some people whose personal conduct is something you cannot approve, yet you could seek their welfare. This is an attitude derived from God. You can do no less than be interested in them. This is the crowning attitude in all we have been considering. Is it not amazing that as we add to godliness brotherly kindness, and to brotherly kindness charity, we have it all?

THE BELIEVER CAN BE FAITHFUL
(2 Peter 1:8-9)

Do you realize that it is possible to have a knowledge of Jesus Christ and still be barren and unfruitful?

> For if these things be in you, and abound, they make you that ye shall neither be barren nor unfruitful in the knowledge of our Lord Jesus Christ. But he that lacketh these things is blind, and cannot see afar off, and hath forgotten that he was purged from his old sins. (2 Peter 1:8-9).

Being a believer in Christ is expected to affect one's manner of life. We think that if a person is a believer, it will show up in what he does. This is not so much in specific acts or deeds. The popular idea that when you speak of a believer in Christ you are speaking of a certain way of doing things can be misleading.

Let us take the life of Jesus of Nazareth. Of all the things He did during the time He was here upon earth we recognize that dying on the cross was His outstanding action as the Christ. Yet dying on the cross was not peculiar to Jesus. On that very day two other men died; He was crucified between two thieves. In that era it was the common mode of execution. What made that cross significant and unique as the cross of Christ? Going to the cross was for Him a voluntary act, and He did it for me. He did not have to go for Himself. He could have escaped it. Pilate tried to get Him out of there, giving Jesus every chance He needed to escape the death sentence. Before that, when Peter wanted to defend Him, Jesus said, "Knowest thou not that I could now ask the Father and I could have twelve legions of angels?" What made going to the cross for Him so necessary, was His attitude, His spirit. So we say with reference to the conduct of a believer in Christ: the believer will not do much differently in outward action from other people in the community. Many who are not believers in Christ give to the Community Chest. This does not mean that giving to the poor is wrong. Giving to the poor is always good, but a believer can give to the poor to the glory of God.

Our particular portion of study is verses 8 and 9, and if a person has the qualities discussed in verses 5, 6, and 7 he "shall neither be barren nor unfruitful in the knowledge of our Lord Jesus Christ. But he that lacketh these things is blind, and cannot see afar off, and hath forgotten that he was purged from his old sins." It is possible to be a believer and yet actually forget it. This is what is referred to here. This does not mean that such a believer will not visit the poor nor contribute to the church, but it does mean that in his experience there will be no love, no joy, no peace. These are the fruits of the Spirit, and they will not be present if the Spirit is not operative.

It may be possible to imitate such actions of a believer and yet to be barren. While I have spoken this way negatively, because that is the way Peter expresses it, I want to comment on what a marvelous promise this is. Just as surely as the Christian believes in God according to the realization of these traits, he will show fruit in his living. Without these traits a person would be blind. Thus a person could be a believer and yet be blind. Is it possible for a believer in Christ to be so short-sighted that he cannot see afar off, and to be unaware that he has been set free? That is what Peter implies here.

When I was a boy on the farm, I learned a great deal about nature watching the horses, cattle, and other creatures. A horse had been shut up for days in a small field. He had wanted to get out of the small enclosure, but he could not. The day came when the farmer took the fence away. But that horse stayed in that little pasture. Why? He did not know the fence was down. There are believers like that; they just do not know that the gate is open. Some believers in Christ are depressed; sometimes it is because of their sins, perhaps past sins. They do not have to carry that burden themselves, but because they think they have to, they keep on living the way they do, at a poor dying rate.

Such people have forgotten that they were purged from their old sins. This expression does not mean the old sins were wiped away and they can now go ahead and sin some more. The old sins were put away when the believer was crucified in Christ; that is the wonderful way the believer is delivered from the old sins. But the tragedy is that a person can accept Christ and actually have all this freedom available, and still not realize it. This will happen if he does not add these attributes Peter has been talking about.

MAKING YOUR CALLING SURE
(2 Peter 1:10)

Do you understand what a believer in Christ could do which would assure him that his experience is real?

> Wherefore the rather, brethren, give diligence to make your calling and election sure: for if ye do these things, ye shall never fall (2 Peter 1:10).

Becoming a believer in Christ is a spiritual matter. It is not visible to the onlooker. And it is not always something about which the believer himself can be absolutely sure. This seems strange. Many people who believe in the Lord Jesus Christ are troubled because they are not "sure" they do believe; they put their trust in the Lord Jesus Christ but they are not sure they are trusting as much as they should. Peter has something important to say: other people should know whether or not you and I really are believers, because it makes a difference to them. They can be blessed by knowing that we truly do believe. Jesus of Nazareth taught that, "by their fruits (by their actions) ye shall know them," and in the same way we will know ourselves. You and I can know for sure that we belong if there are certain things we do. If we leave them undone, it is very hard for us to know. In the wintertime the leaves are off some trees and they look barren. One could wonder which are alive and which are dead. One could not always know. Believers in Christ are like that; if they have no "foliage," so to speak, we do not know whether they are believers or not. If there were no action that would indicate it, one could begin to wonder. When a person wonders whether he belongs or not, it weakens his morale.

In his first epistle John wrote, "We know that we have passed from death unto life, because we love the brethren." Suppose you do not love the brethren, being interested only in yourself. That would be enough to scare you, because you would not have evidence that you belong. Here Peter brings us face to face with a challenging thought: "Wherefore the rather, brethren, give diligence to make your calling and election sure: for if ye do these things, ye shall never fall." Another translation puts it this way: "To make God's call and His choice of you a permanent experience." That would be to say that we should act in such a way that we hear Him all of the time: we do not put our trust in Him once, we trust in Him all the time. Still another version offers these words, "Exert yourselves to clinch God's choice in calling of you." A believer in Christ can do certain things so he will know for sure that he really does belong to God. Still another expresses it like this: "Set your minds then on endorsing by your conduct the fact that God has called and chosen you." You will be acting in such a way that no one will doubt that God has chosen you. Another uses these words, "Be all the more solicitous and eager to make sure your calling and election."

The process of election, God's calling and choosing you, is not selective. In dealing with me God is not looking at other people; He is looking at me. When He gives me a call it is for me to come to Him. If He calls me out of anything, He is not calling me out from my neighbors, He is calling me out from me. Election is a call out of the natural into the spiritual presence of God. The calling of God is the call of the Gospel that He gave to Abraham when He said, "Get thee out of thy country, and from thy kindred, and from thy father's house, unto a land that I will show thee" (Gen. 12:1).

All of this brings to our minds that in the calling of God there is a certain promise offered: "Come out of and I will bring you into." You never come "out of" to be alone; you come "out of" so that you can be free to come "into" what God wants you to do. Now this call, when you hear it in the Gospel, can actually be made real, valid. It can be made ours as we respond to it when we come. This is what Peter is driving home; he says if you have the call of God, put your trust in Him, come close to Him. If you will respond by committing yourself to Him, it will become a part of you. As surely as the believer follows the procedures Peter pointed out, he will exercise self-control, and patience in the will of God, depending upon Him to bring His word to pass. He will in himself live with God; he will have a sense of His presence so that godliness will be in his soul. He will have brotherly kindness and charity. This is the involvement that realizes the promises.

ENTERING THE KINGDOM
(2 Peter 1:11)

Do you realize that a believer in Christ can have more blessing as he is diligent in responding to God's call?

> For so an entrance shall be ministered unto you abundantly into the everlasting kingdom of our Lord and Saviour Jesus Christ (2 Peter 1:11).

In these first few verses of Second Peter the apostle is concerned that believers should enter into the glory and virtue prepared for them. He knows they will do so as they believe in the promises of God in Christ Jesus. A succession of things will happen as they follow through in obedience to Christ. They will, of course, begin with faith. They will be conscious of the reality of God, of what He has done, is doing, and will do; and of what He has promised. They will achieve a certain goodness; their life will be fruitful. There will be virtue and with this they will come to knowledge; they will understand everything better than they did before. In this knowledge of themselves they will be able to achieve in obedience to Christ a certain self-control so that their human natures can be made to serve the Spirit of God. This will lead them to have patience because God is helping them. They will be more and more conscious of the presence of God, and because of this a certain godliness will appear. This will have results: they will be led into kindness to the brethren, and they will be moved with concern for the welfare of other men.

These things are available and possible when a believer follows through in obeying, yielding to, and believing the promises of God that are in Christ Jesus. In verse 11 Peter points out that by following through and obeying the Lord, believers will find that an entrance shall be ministered unto them abundantly into the everlasting kingdom of our Lord and Savior Jesus Christ. Here Peter uses the full name, "our Lord and Savior Jesus Christ." Jesus is the name of His earthly career, the incarnate Son of God, in which He died for sinners. Christ is the name of His office, chosen by God for the work of salvation, which He works in believers. "Savior" draws attention to the function He performs in the sinner: He delivers from sin. Lord refers to the function He performs for the believer: He guides and directs the believer.

"Into the everlasting kingdom of our Lord and Savior Jesus Christ." The word "kingdom" is the term that refers to our relationship with Jesus Christ, He is the King and we are the servants. His dominion extends to us. He rules in our hearts. This is the only relationship possible for us in Christ Jesus. Many times people, in their desire to enter into these things, speak rather comfortably and sometimes intimately and familiarly with the idea of talking to the Lord and of singing the praises of the Lord. They speak of walking with the Lord and begin to look upon Him as a pleasant Companion with whom to walk. Let us remember, however, that He is the Lord.

Let us keep in mind when we talk about walking with the Lord that we are coming into the presence of the One who controls us, who is our King—"the everlasting kingdom." The word "everlasting" means permanent. When we speak of everlasting, everything we see that is real has this element about it.

So entering into fellowship with Him means permanently belonging to Him. "So an entrance shall be ministered unto you." This word "entrance" indicates that the natural man is not in the kingdom of God. He needs to enter into the kingdom of God. Here again this could be misunderstood. A man does not just walk into the kingdom of God, head and shoulders up high. This matter of entering into the kingdom of God is suggested by the way a caterpillar becomes a butterfly, or as a kernel of grain becomes the ripe grain in the field. You sow the seed in the field and the green plant grows, and in the fall of the year it becomes the ripe grain. In this way the seed actually had an "entrance" into being the ripe grain.

This "entrance into the kingdom of God" has to do with moving from natural into spiritual. "Shall be ministered unto you abundantly." This is actually a matter of passing through the death, the burial, and the resurrection of Jesus Christ. This will follow if we diligently do the things that are included in His will, as set forth in His promises, as Peter has been pointing out (2 Peter 1:4). Just as surely as we follow through, this will be done for us. We will actually be translated out of the natural into the spiritual, from the flesh into the spirit, out of this world into that world. We will move from being human into being a child of God. This will be done for us in Christ Jesus.

THE PRESENT TRUTH
(2 Peter 1:12-14)

Do you know how important it is for a believer in Christ to remember what is promised in Christ Jesus?

> Wherefore I will not be negligent to put you always in remembrance of these things, though ye know them, and be established in the present truth. Yea, I think it meet, as long as I am in this tabernacle, to stir you up by putting you in remembrance (2 Peter 1:12-13).

To be valid, faith needs to know what is true about the promises. Faith is not just my attitude of being willing to trust God; it is, rather, knowing what God has promised and believing that to be true; taking that for myself. Taking His Word as real is the way to have the kind of faith that brings the blessing of God. Faith is not something you accomplish in yourself; faith is the matter of reaching up and receiving from God what He has promised. I need to understand and remember what God has promised, and if I will enter into an understanding of these things I can receive them, and they will be mine.

All of the promises of God are yea and amen in Christ Jesus. For this reason it is basically important for the believer in Christ not only to know Jesus Christ as He lived and died and rose again in this world, but to remember these things every day. We are to remember not only that Christ Jesus died for us on Calvary's cross, for which we praise God; but we are to remember the grave into which He was put. We are to remember the resurrection by which He came out, and we are to remember the Ascension into heaven in full view of a whole number of disciples. We are to remember His present intercession on our behalf and His coming again to receive us unto Himself. It is as the Christian believes these things that the blessing of God comes upon him. When the Lord Jesus Christ said, "He that hath seen me hath seen the Father," He was not referring to His appearance as you would see Him in a picture. The person who understands what happened in Jesus of Nazareth (God in human form), His taking that form to the cross, lifting that form out of the grave, raising that form into the full newness of life, living in that form with God, coming in that form again, understands that God will work in him that same kind of thing.

Since Christ Jesus appeared once in history (and anything that happened once can be forgotten since we human beings are quick to forget many things) the facts of His life need to be told over and over again. In that way the Holy Spirit can prepare the believer to receive blessing. In these verses Peter writes these things so that believers can remember them, "and be established in the present truth."

> Yea, I think it meet, as long as I am in this tabernacle, to stir you up by putting you in remembrance; knowing that shortly I must put off this my tabernacle, even as our Lord Jesus Christ hath showed me (2 Peter 1:13-14).

Peter does this by writing to the believers; not by writing

another Gospel, but by writing about the meaning of these things. We shall find in this epistle certain things that will remind the believers. The wonderful thing is that his letter can be read at any time, today, tomorrow, or a month from now, to "put you always in remembrance of these things." This expression, "and be established in the present truth," is significant. It could have been translated thus: "Firmly fixed in the truth that you have received." Or it could have been expressed in this way: "Well grounded in the truth that has already reached you." Again it could have been said, "You are already established in the truth." That is the "present" aspect. Because you have believed some things, more is coming; but this much is true.

Again, the experience of the believer was like an apple tree in the orchard. You may not see apples on it as yet, but they will come; and it is still an apple tree. Someone may say, "Who do you think you are?" And you might humbly say, "I think I am a child of God." And he will say, "Where do you think you are going?" You could say, "I think I am going to heaven. Right now I am not in heaven, but I believe in Him; and that is the present truth I have. Other things are coming." In verse 13 we see that Peter felt it was his responsibility to stir up the believers by putting them in remembrance. Peter knew he would not live much longer, and when he speaks of his tabernacle he is speaking of his natural body (it was like a tent, not permanent), "Even as our Lord Jesus Christ hath showed me."

Those who know the Gospel have a responsibility to share with others who do not know the Gospel. This is what Peter felt.

PETER'S TESTIMONY WAS TRUE
(2 Peter 1:15-16)

Have you ever noticed that the strongest argument for the reality of the Gospel of Christ is in the personal testimony of a soul that has been blessed?

> Moreover I will endeavor that ye may be able after my decease
> to have these things always in remembrance. For we have not
> followed cunningly devised fables, when we made known unto
> you the power and coming of our Lord Jesus Christ, but were
> eyewitnesses of his majesty (2 Peter 1:15-16).

Peter proposed to undertake certain helpful measures that would aid the memory of people who were reading his epistle. He felt he could do this because of his own vivid experiences. In the above verses he gave guidance for them that they might enter into reality of these things, because he was actually there. I am interested in the way he refers to his death, "That ye may be able after my decease to have these things always in remembrance." Peter was able to speak about this objectively. Apparently it did not upset him in any emotional way at all. All of us know that we will not stay here forever, although we cannot estimate for how long. Peter was an older man; and he knew his death would soon occur. With this in mind he made plans as to what should be done after he was gone. Peter seemed to consider his own passing away just an event in the common battle for the spread of the Gospel.

While he was in this earthly tabernacle he could do some definite, positive things, so that they might always have this material before them. One of the things he did was to write the Scripture for which he was responsible. One reason why Peter wanted to do this, and why he felt so confident and really commissioned to do this, was because he had been an eye witness to Jesus Christ in the flesh.

Here is a phrase that has been often quoted: "For we have not followed cunningly devised fables." The entire world of believers has been seriously disturbed in recent years by some important people who have cleverly proposed that the writers of Scripture told stories to illustrate their ideas. They say that when you read the incidents that are recorded both in the Old and New Testaments, you should not take them as real or historical; you should take them as fables or myths, understanding that they are just stories to illustrate the real truths. However, Peter could not have said it more plainly when he made this statement, "We have not followed cunningly devised fables, when we made known unto you the power and coming of our Lord Jesus Christ"—the power which is to be seen in the resurrection, and the coming which is to be seen both in Pentecost and in His coming again.

"But were eyewitnesses of his majesty." Nobody can shake the testimony of an eyewitness. When I first became a believer in Christ I remember what a shock it was to me to hear a man say seriously that he believed Jesus Christ was alive. I asked him how he knew that Jesus Christ was alive. The old man said, with a smile, "I have dealings with Him every day." What an answer that was! Let us recall from this passage that believers are to remember the facts of the life of the Lord Jesus Christ as they are recorded. The report that they read in the Bible is real and actual. These things did happen just exactly that way, as they are reported.

THE VOICE FROM HEAVEN
(2 Peter 1:17-18)

Do you think the Bible really means to say that a voice was heard from heaven by the apostle?

> For he received from God the Father honour and glory, when there came such a voice to him from the excellent glory, This is my beloved Son, in whom I am well pleased. And this voice which came from heaven we heard, when we were with him in the holy mount (2 Peter 1:17-18)

No one can read the Gospels without feeling that suddenly the windows of heaven are opened and one is made to stand in the very presence of God, to even hear the very voice of God. You will see the power of God demonstrated in miracles that are performed before your eyes. When you read the Gospels—Matthew, Mark, Luke, and John—you will know that Jesus of Nazareth as He lived and walked in this world was actually the Son of God. Just now Peter is pointing out that he heard an actual voice from heaven at the Mount of Transfiguration, where he, James, and John went up with Jesus. We have Peter's description of this in verses 17 and 18, and we read about it in the Gospels.

Peter wanted the people who were reading his epistle to know that the things they had heard about Jesus Christ were real, and they will be real in you, wherever you may be. Did you notice that Peter does not refer to anything remarkable that Jesus Christ did? He refers to honor and glory that were given to Him from God. This idea is presented over and over again in the Bible. Blessing is something that is given to you from God. If you are burdened let me tell you: you can have blessing; you can have joy, even though you have no strength. You can be inwardly helped and strengthened. You have only to open your heart and receive from God what He will give to you. After you receive blessing from God you will walk and not faint, you will run and not be weary, because God Himself will carry you. When the Lord Jesus was here upon earth the great blessing in His life came to Him as a gift from His Father in heaven. It was given to Him when there came a voice to Him from the excellent glory. I first heard this when my own son preached on this passage while attending seminary. I was thrilled to realize that he had seen something like this. He pointed out that most people remember Peter because of the times when he blundered and stumbled, but not all remember that Peter is the man who was with the Lord Jesus Christ on the Mount of Transfiguration. He saw some wonderful things about the Lord, who dealt with Peter faithfully and graciously. And Peter heard these words, "When there came such a voice to him from the excellent glory, This is my beloved Son, in whom I am well pleased."

There is much skepticism today. The common disposition of people is generally not to believe, and this skepticism hinders faith. We grow as we receive and enter into the precious promises. We need to get to know them in the knowledge of Jesus Christ. This knowledge comes as we learn the event of His life, like this voice from heaven. If, at that point, you back off and do not go right through to believe, then you can mark that spot, because from that time on your spiritual life will not grow. The skepticism that does not receive and does not believe hinders faith. It reduces the testimony of the Scriptures to something useless.

The Word is plain. Men may question and men may deny, but the record stands. There is another world besides this one. God is in heaven. Jesus Christ knew Him and can bring us to His Father in heaven, for which we thank the Lord.

THE WORD OF PROPHECY IS A LIGHT
(2 Peter 1:19-20)

Do you know how the ideas of the Bible can be made more convincing?

> We have also a more sure word of prophecy; whereunto ye do well that ye take heed, as unto a light that shineth in a dark place, until the day dawn, and the day star arise in your hearts: knowing this first, that no prophecy of the scripture is of any private interpretation (2 Peter 1:19-20).

This is a very important passage. It points out that if you will accept the events that happened in the earthly career of Jesus of Nazareth certain fruits will appear to the glory of God.

The Old Testament history, which occurred over a thousand years during the time of Israel, revealed certain promises and predicted events concerning the Messiah, the Christ, who was to come to save His people. The Son of God came and fulfilled those predictions. To accept that He fulfilled them is to be strengthened in your personal faith. "We have also a more sure word of prophecy." How can the ideas in the Bible be made more convincing? Another translation expresses this by saying, "So we are even more confident of the message." Still another version puts it, "All this only confirms for us the message of the prophets," speaking especially about the things that happened to Jesus of Nazareth in the course of His lifetime, such as the Transfiguration. And again another scholar says, "The word of prophecy was fulfilled in our hearing." So we become more confident because it was fulfilled. When things promised in the Old Testament actually happened to Jesus, the message that it contains is commended to us. This seems to be the meaning of the passage that says we have a more sure word of prophecy; so we can study the promises and learn from them with confidence.

Peter thinks of the Scripture as light shining in a dark place, like a lantern at night, the dark place being this world "until the day dawn." I suggest that the day dawns for any one of us when we see the glory of God in the face of Jesus Christ. "And the day star arise in your hearts," I suggest this would be the work of the Holy Spirit. This indicates that the Scripture is like a lantern leading you along a dark place, bringing you closer into the understanding of the truth.

"Knowing this first, that no prophecy of the scripture is of any private interpretation." Another translation says, "No one can by himself explain a prophecy of scripture." I am inclined to think that means without any evidence. If you study any passage by itself alone you will never really understand a prophecy of Scripture. Bring in other Scriptures so you can understand events as they happened. One scholar says this means, "No one can interpret any prophecy of scripture by himself"; while still another says, "No prophecy arose from an individual's interpretation of the truth." We compare Scripture with Scripture and then look for results. In this way we strengthen our confidence and come to grasp the whole truth. The Scriptures are given for our guidance. But more than to understand the letter of the word, we are to come into personal fellowship with God through the Lord Jesus Christ.

THE ORIGIN OF SCRIPTURE
(2 Peter 1:21)

Do you realize whenever you hear a sincere preacher of the Gospel that you are hearing a man who was sent to preach?

> For the prophecy came not in old time by the will of man: but holy men of God spake as they were moved by the Holy Ghost (2 Peter 1:21).

Peter urges believers to take heed of the Old Testament Scripture for their spiritual welfare. He emphasizes these things that they might be strong in their personal response to the Lord. Peter pointed out that the Old Testament had been confirmed by events, and thus the Word was made sure. In this last verse of this chapter he argues that the origin of the Scriptures testified to their authenticity. Scripture did not come by the will of man; men like Isaiah and Jeremiah did not preach because they were students of society and had good ideas; these men were sent. "Holy men of God spake as they were moved by the Holy Ghost."

I suspect many men go into the ministry because they have ideas they would like to share with people, or perhaps a man may feel that if he will read and study he can come up with good ideas. That is not the way the holy men of old preached. They spake as they were moved by the Holy Ghost. We need not be afraid of the word "holy." Every believer in Christ is told to be holy, for God is holy. The word "holy" really comes from the English word "whole" and so it means those holy men of God were entirely committed; their thinking was not clouded with selfish thoughts. Those holy men were moved, inwardly pressed into action by the Holy Ghost. This word "Ghost" is also used for the word "Spirit"; these are interchangeable words, having the same meaning.

How would the Holy Ghost move a man—like the wind moves the trees, or like a man moves a chair? Is it a "push or pull"? No; rather it is by showing him things. The Holy Spirit moves me by showing me the things of Christ. Showing me what He has done for me can move me to a certain action of gratitude toward Him. Showing me what Christ Jesus is now doing for me, interceding for me in heaven, is comforting and encouraging. Showing me what the Lord Jesus can do for me can incline me to walk that way. If I know that the living Lord Jesus Christ will tomorrow guide me in His will, I want to do what is pleasing in His sight today. In this way the Holy Spirit will guide.

So these men of God in the Old Testament uttered, they wrote, as they were moved by the Holy Spirit of God. This is the origin of Scripture. Because the Bible came to pass in this way Peter would say we should pay special attention to it. The Scripture is not the word of man; it came from God and is for you. It will strengthen and guide you. You and I can have no better word about the Scriptures than that they are in our hands today because holy men of God wrote as they were moved by the Holy Ghost.

SECOND PETER
Chapter 2

† † †

THERE WILL BE FALSE PROPHETS
(2 Peter 2:1-2)

Can you understand that having weeds in the garden is not good for it?

> But there were false prophets also among the people, even as there shall be false teachers among you, who privily shall bring in damnable heresies, even denying the Lord that bought them, and bring upon themselves swift destruction. And many shall follow their pernicious ways; by reason of whom the way of truth shall be evil spoken of (2 Peter 2:1-2).

Peter is writing this urgent letter to believers in Christ that they might follow through in their believing fellowship with the Lord Jesus Christ, that they might bear fruit to the glory of His name, and that they might share in the wonderful blessing of the Spirit of God. He ended his first chapter by urging them to pay special attention to the Word of God.

Many things in the world are strange and seem unnecessary. As a boy I wondered why there are mosquitoes; they did not do any work, you could not eat them, and they bothered you. If God made the heavens and the earth and everything in it, why did He make mosquitoes? When I became older I wondered why He made flies. As I have grown older and seen things around me and understand better, I could raise the question: why did the Lord God make disease germs? I do not know. I do not know why there are thistles and thorns, and weeds in the gardens. While it is true in the natural world that weeds grow in gardens, it is just as true in the spiritual world that weeds grow in the garden of the heart and consciousness. In the natural world, thieves break through and steal; foxes run away with your chickens; and forces will destroy things. So it is true in the spiritual world that there are those who are active contrary to the things of the Gospel. For every good procedure in spiritual living, for every valid promise in the Gospel, there are alternatives that will lead you astray. The soul of man is confronted by substitutes. Whenever you hear a clear call from God there will be another almost like it. These substitutes come to you as if they were just as good.

This line of truth is very sobering and Peter dwelt on it here. "There were false prophets also among the people." False prophets are those who offered ideas that were different from those of the true prophet, and oftentimes these ideas were offered as practical and more convenient. The ideas were false not so much because these men were liars. Oftentimes they had false ideas even when they were sincere in their own intentions. The ideas were false in the sense that they led the wrong way.

Most of us know what it is to be traveling and get to a place where we do not know which road to take. When we stopped to ask someone, he directed us to a road that was wrong; he may have thought it was the right road, but he was a false guide. The way he pointed out did not get us where we wanted to go. That is the way it was with the false prophets. There are repeated warnings in Scripture about this. We are not born with a knowledge of God; we have to depend on others to teach us and to show us. This is the kind of world where people will show us the wrong things. These false teachers among you, "who privily (secretly, furtively) shall bring in damnable heresies."

If all heresies looked bad they would not be so dangerous. All heresies that ever get anywhere in themselves look good, because any heresy, to be really a heresy, is half true. In other words, a man can tell you much that is true and still lead you astray. He can tell you a certain road is good, and it may be. He can say it is a road people travel on, and that may be true. But that does not necessarily mean it will take you where you want to go. Such guidance is dangerous because it is partly true.

These heresies should be condemned because they are "even denying the Lord that bought them." What does that mean? There are members of churches who do not depend on the death of Christ for their salvation; they depend on their good works. They do not claim to follow Him; they follow their own judgment. Do you realize they are denying the Lord?

You may hear any number of men preaching what you ought to do, but you seldom hear anything from them to the glory of the name of Jesus Christ as One who died for you. They will speak of Him as someone you should follow, but not as One who died for you. We need to remember the Lord bought us with His own precious blood on Calvary's cross.

"And many shall follow their pernicious ways," not "pernicious" because these ways look bad or feel bad, but because they lead you astray. Such leaders are a bad influence. Many follow them. "Broad is the way that leadeth unto destruction, many there be that go in thereat." "By reason of whom the way of truth shall be evil spoken of." Now this is serious and it is very important that you and I know about it. Those who teach things that are not true do not honor the Lord Jesus Christ.

THE WORK OF FALSE TEACHERS
(2 Peter 2:3)

Have you ever felt that someone interpreting Scripture was really interested in winning support for his own personal program?

> And through covetousness shall they with feigned words make merchandise of you: whose judgment now of a long time lingereth not, and their damnation slumbereth not (2 Peter 2:3).

Peter now began to question the integrity of these false teachers. He pointed out that many of them would try to take advantage of their hearers. These teachers will actually make merchandise of their pupils, trying to make a profit from them. We must notice that God allows substitutes to be offered to us who would mislead us. In other words, in this world there is food, and by food we live; but also in this world there is poison, and by poison we die. Over and over again we are faced with the fact that something other than that which is right may be offered to us, often made very attractive in the offer. Trusting in God is essential. It seems as though God allows these questionable things to be presented as a sort of test, so that we should have a choice. Thus the person who can be appealed to for selfish reasons will find something other than God's will that he may want to do.

God's will is revealed in His Word, but God demands humility on my part that I may see it. Repentance is also required. I need to recognize that my conduct is not what it should be at all times. Humility and repentance are prerequisites to walking with and being blessed by God. God allows substitutes to be offered in which it will be suggested that I can achieve the things I want, and I will not need to be humble. I can actually feel somewhat proud of myself. This is a deception, and here I can make my mistake. The heart can be affected by flattery and promise of gain. We seek attention, and it is a temptation to accept the false teachings. Oftentimes honesty hurts people, and many times false teachers will not be strictly honest, but will use flattery and promise of gain.

God allows these false teachers to actually fabricate what they present in order to get our attention and to get our approval of what they promote. Peter is harsh in his warning, and it might be helpful to read other translations of this passage in order to learn that the King James Version has actually a good standard of accuracy in translation. One other translation presents this verse like this, "In their greed these false teachers will make a profit out of telling you made-up stories. For a long time now their Judge has been ready, and their Destroyer has been wide awake!" Another translation expresses it this way, "In their greed for money they will trade on your credulity with sheer fabrication but the judgment long decreed for them has not been idle, perdition waits for them with unsleeping eyes." This is a stern warning. We read in still another translation, "In their lust to make converts these men will try to exploit you too with their bogus arguments, but judgment has been for some time hard on their heels and their downfall is inevitable." And once again another version is, "In their convetousness they will exploit you with (cunning) false arguments. From of old the sentence (of condemnation) for them has not been idle; their destruction (eternal misery) has not been asleep."

Remember, when the teacher wants something that you can give to him, perhaps your support, or your vote, you should be very careful. "With feigned words," the word "feign" is just as it sounds: dishonest. "Make merchandise of you." They will treat you as if you were something to be bought and sold. "Whose judgment now of a long time lingereth not, and their damnation slumbereth not." God will punish them at the right time. If we are honest with ourselves we need not fear anything; but if we allow ourselves to be flattered into being presumptuous before God, we are in danger.

THE DESTRUCTION OF THE WICKED
(2 Peter 2:4-5)

Do you realize the Bible reveals that God will destroy in judgment?

> For if God spared not the angels that sinned, but cast them down to hell, and delivered them into chains of darkness, to be reserved unto judgment; and spared not the old world, but saved Noah the eighth person, a preacher of righteousness, bringing in the flood upon the world of the ungodly (2 Peter 2:4-5).

This statement is almost incredible to the public mind. People who admit that they know nothing about God will say that God would never destroy anything. Such are mistaken, and it is strange they say that when all about them is destruction. Think of such an innocent thing as grass; it withers. Flowers fade, trees become infested with insects, and so on, all through nature, and even among human beings. We see many persons suffering in ways they do not deserve, having trouble they did not cause.

The Bible teaches that God will destroy deliberately those who are not in His will. The Bible reveals God as a God of judgment. Other translations may prove helpful, since modern translations sometimes translate more vividly and even more harshly than the King James Version does. One reads thus, "God did not spare the angels who sinned, but threw them into hell, where they are kept chained in darkness, waiting for the day of judgment. God did not spare the ancient world but brought the flood on the world of godless men: the only ones he saved were Noah, who preached righteousness, and seven other people." Another translation words this passage in this way: "God did not spare the angels who sinned, but consigned them to the dark pits of hell where they are reserved for judgment. He did not spare the world of old, except for Noah, a preacher of righteousness whom He preserved with seven others, but brought the deluge upon that world of godless men."

In still another it is written, "For if God did not spare angels who sinned against him, but banished them to the dark imprisonment of hell until judgment day, if he did not spare the ancient world but saved only Noah, the solitary voice that cried out for righteousness and his seven companions when he brought the flood upon the world in its wickedness." And again it is written, "For God (even) spared not angels that sinned, but cast them into hell, delivering them to be kept there in pits of gloom till the judgment and their doom. And He spared not the ancient world, but preserved Noah, a preacher of righteousness, with seven other persons, when He brought a flood upon the world of ungodly (people)."

God will use hell to destroy, in darkness and in doom. Every translation used that word "hell." Men may preach and never use the word, but the Bible does. We also learn that God will spare. A person can be saved. God will save those who seek righteousness.

Peter is predicting destruction, not just upon all sinners, although it will come upon all sinners, but he is predicting this destruction for teachers who mislead believers. Jesus of Nazareth revealed the judgment of God upon people who mislead others.

> But whoso shall offend one of these little ones which believe in me, it were better for him that a millstone were hanged about his neck, and that he were drowned in the depth of the sea (Matt. 18:6).

John writes:

> And I saw an angel come down from heaven, having the key of the bottomless pit and a great chain in his hand. And he laid hold on the dragon, that old serpent, which is the Devil, and Satan,

and bound him a thousand years, and cast him into the bottom-less pit (Rev. 20:1-3).

The Bible makes this plain: God will destroy the wicked.

THE CLASSIC EXAMPLE OF DESTRUCTION
(2 Peter 2:6)

Have you ever wondered if the cities of Sodom and Gomorrah were actually destroyed by fire?

> And turning the cities of Sodom and Gomorrah into ashes condemned them with an overthrow, making them an example unto those that after should live ungodly (2 Peter 2:6).

This is part of a passage in which Peter is saying some very sober things about the reality of God's judgment. In order that the believers might be strong in faith he offered several considerations: they should remember that they had not followed cunningly devised fables; that the stories told about Jesus Christ were real; and that events described in those stories were actually events in history. Things would be written, and things told, in the stories that would reach beyond this world, which Peter urged believers to remember. He himself had heard the voice from heaven; and if they would believe what he had been telling them, they would enter into more and more knowledge of the Lord Jesus Christ. But even beyond what he wrote, they had other Scriptures which would interpret these things to them.

Peter says that someone is going to explain the Scriptures. Philip asked the Ethiopian riding along in his chariot, "Understandest thou what thou readest?" And the Ethiopian said, "How can I, except some man should guide me?" This is always true. Those who know must show the people who do not know. It is wonderfully true that, "Whosoever shall call on the name of the Lord shall be saved," but it follows, "How then shall they call on him in whom they have not believed? and how shall they believe in him of whom they have not heard? and how shall they hear without a preacher?" (Rom. 10:14).

Peter mentions that they will have teachers, but he also gives a serious word of warning. Apparently he is afraid some will know the Gospel and not do anything about it, so Peter urges believers to be careful about the kind of teaching to which they listen. He speaks about the false teachers among them, whom we have noted. This passage brings to mind something that should be emphasized, "And turning the cities of Sodom and Gomorrah into ashes condemned them with an overthrow, making them an example unto those that after should live ungodly." Was the story in Genesis historical? Some readers wonder about the historicity of certain events in the Bible. Some of these events are referred to in Second Peter. Here in verse 5 we have the story of Noah and the ark, and how God sent the flood to destroy the old world. In verse 6 we have reference to Sodom and Gomorrah. Later on in the same chapter we shall have the story of the prophet Balaam and the ass speaking to him. Peter brings these exceptional occurrences before the believers, calling upon them not to shrink back from the Word of God, but to note especially these things.

Let us look more closely at this matter of Sodom and Gomorrah. The King James Version says, "turning the cities of Sodom and Gomorrah into ashes." In another translation these words are used: "Destroying them with fire and made an example of them for the wicked of what will happen to them." In another passage we read, "God turned to ashes, making them an object lesson for godless men in future days." Still another translation reads, "God reduced the entire cities to ashes as a fearful example," while another says, "He condemned to ruin and extinction these cities, reducing them to ashes as an example." Let me again raise the question; will God destroy disobedient, unresponsive men? Will He destroy the godless, those who live their lives away from God? And the answer, based upon the Scriptures, is: He will. This teaching should be heeded. The people in the cities of Sodom and Gomorrah were willing to live as if there were no God. But God exists, and any man is a fool to live as if there were no God. Those people were foolish and God made an example of them. Throughout all Scripture, both the Old and New Testaments, right to this very time, the cities of Sodom and Gomorrah are forever a classic example of the fact that God will destroy disobedient, unresponsive, ungodly men. What happened to them is to be taken as a warning of what can happen to anybody who lives as they did. Believers in Christ should respond to the truth. They should be concerned, both for themselves and for others, that they really enter into the spiritual truth of the Gospel, because it is a matter of life and death.

THE FOOLISHNESS OF LOT
(2 Peter 2:7-8)

Could a believer in Christ ever be willing to accept ungodly practices where he lives?

> And delivered just Lot, vexed with the filthy conversation of the wicked: (for that righteous man dwelling among them, in seeing and hearing, vexed his righteous soul from day to day with their unlawful deeds) (2 Peter 2:7-8).

In writing this epistle Peter, as brought out before, had believing people in mind. In this chapter he gives a warning. In the first place, error is obviously possible. One can actually respond to preaching in a way that is not sound: receiving in the ears the word from the Scriptures and not responding in the heart; thereby missing the blessing. Now part of this is because of the teachers. What many people learn about God, they hear from others who have read the Bible, and then they study for themselves. That is always best, and in that way faith becomes stronger. The believer grows in the grace and in the knowledge of the Lord Jesus Christ, bearing fruit to the glory of His Name.

This is what Peter wanted, and he wrote this book as advice to believers. In it we find the strong exhortation that they should beware unsound teaching. Many of us have the tendency to feel that once a person has accepted Christ Jesus as Savior he will have no further problem. His sins are forgiven for Christ's sake. But there is more to the relationship with the Lord Jesus Christ than receiving and acknowledging Him. There is also the need to obey Him and follow Him.

Peter's emphasis upon the danger of error is a warning that believers could lose their blessing. They can lose by listening to the wrong teachers; those who do not lead through into obedience. He is warning that God's judgment is real. God will judge these teachers and also those who follow them. In verses 7 and 8 Peter reminds them about what God did, "And delivered just Lot, vexed with the filthy conversation of the wicked: for that righteous man dwelling among them, in seeing and hearing, vexed his righteous soul from day to day with their unlawful deeds." When Peter wrote that God delivered just Lot he did not mean "just" in the sense of "only" Lot; that word "just" is like the word "righteous." Some may think only Lot was delivered, but his wife and two daughters were also delivered.

We should be careful how we judge others. When I read about Lot in the Old Testament I am not inclined to think of him as a righteous man. But according to the Scriptures, he was counted as a righteous man because he believed in God. Yet he lost much. Lot lived in Sodom, but he did not live with the people of Sodom; he did not behave as they did. Lot's career is a strange one, which should be a lesson for many of us. He started as a fellow believer with his uncle Abraham, and the two of them came from Ur of the Chaldees. When the time came that Abraham and Lot separated because of trouble over their flocks and their servants, Lot chose to risk living in the plains that were near Sodom, an extremely wicked city. What a warning that is! Lot was willing to take certain action even though he knew he was getting close to wickedness. It was a case of playing with fire, and many have found that in playing with fire one can get burned.

This happened once in my own pastoral experience. A man in my church apparently had an earnest desire to know and be with God. He was successful in business. Because he had made much money, he moved from the community where he lived into a sophisticated community with high-priced homes. The subsequent story of that man's life was clouded by the fact that both his wife and daughters became worldly and his whole life thereafter, instead of being spiritual, became instead an association with people who were after money and pleasure.

This apparently happened with Lot. He was "vexed with the filthy conversation of the ungodly people," and even though he was in a place he should not be, he did not give in. For this reason, perhaps, he was delivered. He lost his property; it was burned up in the city. He lost his wife; she turned back. And he lost his honor. It is disastrous to live near the ungodly, just as it is wonderful to be saved by the power of God.

GOD CAN DELIVER THE GODLY
(2 Peter 2:9)

Can you understand that God will permit trouble to come to a believer in Christ, and at the same time be ready and able to deliver him out of that trouble?

> The Lord knoweth how to deliver the godly out of temptations, and to reserve the unjust unto the day of judgment to be punished (2 Peter 2:9).

This is just one simple statement, but we find it very profound. It is the testimony of the whole Bible. In our last study Peter commented on Lot and his deliverance. Lot is an example of a real believer who was involved in a worldly situation. Here is what Paul wrote to the Corinthians along this line:

> There hath no temptation taken you but such as is common to man: but God is faithful, who will not suffer you to be tempted above that ye are able; but will with the temptation also make a way to escape, that ye may be able to bear it (1 Cor. 10:13).

God has His eye upon His people and when they get into situations where there is trouble, God will arrange for them to get out of it.

This word "temptation" has a broader meaning than being enticed by something wrong. Some other translations simply use the word "trial" and say the Lord knoweth how to deliver the godly when he is surrounded by trial, or testing. A common word for temptation is the word "trouble." All of us realize the truth in the old saying that troubles never come singly. The Bible says in one place that man is born to trouble as the sparks fly upward. Jesus of Nazareth said that in the world you shall have tribulation; that means trouble. Jesus had trouble, and you and I will have trouble, not always because we are doing wrong, or are out of the will of God.

There is real promise in the word that Peter wrote: The Lord can deliver. When we read "the Lord knoweth how" it implies that escape from trouble is not simple, and it is not sure, nor is it inevitable. There is a way to escape which the Lord will provide, "and to reserve the unjust unto the day of judgment to be punished." This is where Peter shows us the other side of the coin. Some people are godly. And some people are unjust (which is a way of saying they are ungodly, unrighteous). Did you notice the difference? The deliverance for the godly is now; while you are involved you can be delivered. The punishment of the wicked is later; it comes on the day of judgment.

Now this sometimes is a bit confusing, because if we do wrong certain results seem to follow immediately. For instance, if a man drives carelessly he might have a collision; if you leave the door open flies will come in. Results that follow immediately are not so much in the nature of punishment. Punishment comes because you did wrong; it is especially imposed upon you, not just something implicit in the act itself. A day will come when God will actually deal with those who have done wrong. But this is not the day of judgment.

People studying the Bible at different times and in different ways have pointed out that this is the day of grace, the day when God specializes on one great truth: "Come unto me, all ye that labour and are heavy laden, and I will give you rest" (Matt. 11:28). "Look unto me, and be ye saved, all the ends of the earth: for I am God, and there is none else" (Isa. 45:22). The promise is that anybody can come; and whosoever comes, God will receive. This does not mean God does not see the wrongdoers. He knows them, but He is not dealing with them now. They will be punished on the day of judgment. We often think it would be simpler if the punishment were immediate; this is our natural response. Do you remember the parable of the wheat and the tares? When the servants saw the weeds growing among the wheat, they asked the master if they should pull the weeds out. But the master said, "Let them both grow together until the harvest." Psalm 73 is a classic meditation upon this problem. In mercy and grace God will spare the righteous and He will hold off the punishment of the wicked, but not forever. Punishment will come later. It is true and sure.

SCOFFERS ARE CONDEMNED
(2 Peter 2:10)

Do you realize that God takes particular note of persons who scorn spiritual matters?

> But chiefly them that walk after the flesh in the lust of uncleanness, and despise government. Presumptuous are they, self-willed, they are not afraid to speak evil of dignities (2 Peter 2:10).

Some persons do not believe the Gospel is true; some believe it is true but they are not willing to respond. They are not ready for it. There are some who not only do not believe, they despise and ridicule those who do. Peter is here referring to this latter group. Unfortunately such persons often appear among public speakers, commentators, teachers, and sometimes even preachers.

I grew up as an unbeliever. I went to Sunday school and church and was among good people, but somehow the truth of the Gospel never seemed to get into the consciousness of my heart. I did not realize I was missing anything. I knew something was lacking in me, but I did not know it was in the Gospel and that I would find it through the Bible. After I became a believer in Christ and was teaching school as a young man, I met my first atheist, a farmer in Saskatchewan. He let it be known that he did not believe there was a God. He and I had repeated discussions. I do not know whether anyone ever won him, but I knew from then on what that frame of mind is like.

Later, when I began to prepare myself for what I thought would be my work on the mission field, I was in the Bible Institute of Los Angeles. One of our exercises was to preach the Gospel to the public anywhere we could under supervision; part of this was street preaching. I met many skeptics, atheists, and agnostics. In more recent years, to my great sorrow, I have found the same frame of mind among people who claim to be believers in Christ. I even encountered it in some of my seminary students. I have heard ministers give the impression they despise spiritual things. Some people, associated with churches in various ways, actually belittle prayer. They do not object to it as a public exercise, a sort of deferential tipping of the hat to God. But as for spending time in prayer, they ridicule that, claiming it is only for the psychological compensation people get out of it.

Peter knows there are such persons in the world and that believers in Christ must face them. In this epistle he tells believers that these arrogant, presumptuous, insulting persons, who think nothing wrong of deriding spiritual matters, will be dealt with by God. The Lord knows how to reserve the unjust unto the day of judgment to be punished. This verse has been translated, "Especially those who follow their filthy bodily lusts and despise God's authority." Now when the words "uncleanness" and "filthy" are used, one naturally thinks of something immoral, crude, or vulgar, but it could mean more. Pride is a filthy thing with God; the selfishness of man is unclean with God. "These false teachers are bold and arrogant, and show no respect for the glorious beings above; instead, they insult them." If you mention angels, such persons will laugh; if you mention heaven, they will just smile.

Another translation has been made: "Above all he will punish those who follow their abominable lusts. They flout authority; reckless and headstrong, they are not afraid to insult celestial beings." In still another we read, "His judgment is chiefly reserved for those who have indulged all the foulness of their lower natures and have nothing but contempt for authority. These men are arrogant and presumptuous, they think nothing of scoffing at the glories of the unseen world."

Here is a description of how a person can be when he is opposed to the things of the Lord: "And particularly those who walk after the flesh and indulge in the lust of polluting passion, and scorn and despise authority. Presumptuous and daring— self-willed and self-loving. They scoff at and revile dignitaries without trembling." Why is Peter telling the believers this? To warn them. We should be careful to whom we listen; be careful what books we read. We need to be careful of the comments we listen to, and we should remember this: God knows all about these people and in His own good time He will deal with them in judgment.

THE CALLOUS NATURE OF FALSE PROPHETS
(2 Peter 2:11-12)

Have you ever noticed that often the person who understands the least talks the most?

> Whereas angels, which are greater in power and might, bring not railing accusation against them before the Lord. But these, as natural brute beasts, made to be taken and destroyed, speak evil of the things that they understand not; and shall utterly perish in their own corruption (2 Peter 2:11-12).

Believers in Christ are among the first to acknowledge that they do not know everything. They are also inclined to be humble. This makes them ready to listen, but at the same time this causes immediately a great danger. As soon as they are ready to listen, someone is ready to talk. Here we should note a word of warning from Scripture: take heed how you hear. The Bible speaks of this in different places. Be careful to whom you listen, and whom you read. Peter warns believers in Christ against false teachers.

You will notice that though he has spoken very plainly, Peter never does name any individual. I am sure he could have named them, but he did not. And although he speaks of them bringing in damnable heresies, he does not describe their errors. This is a profound scriptural, biblical New Testament principle. In his epistles the apostle Paul actually contended with people who had wrong ideas, but you will read his writings in vain if you are seeking to find out specifically what these false teachers said. We can learn much from that. Peter does definitely warn against false leaders and their way of misleading, but he gives no additional information.

In our last study we noted that Peter pointed out the arrogant, contemptuous way some teachers discredit spiritual matters. Now in this portion of Scripture Peter contrasts their contemptuous way of doing things with the conduct of angels. He pointed out that the angels, who are much greater in power, would not speak of those false teachers in as belittling a way as the false teachers refer to angels. Angels are much stronger, yet they are more careful—a profound spiritual principle. Peter speaks of these persons as being natural animals who actually have no significant status in creation. Another translation says, "But these men act by instinct," and that is what is meant by calling them brute beasts, animals. They act by instinct, " . . . like wild animals born to be captured and killed."

In the covenant that God made with Noah (see Genesis 9:2-3), God told Noah that the fear of him and the dread of him would be upon the whole of creation. Both plant life and animal life was given over to man to use for food, which means these animals could be killed for food. Apparently natural animals have no individual significant status so far as creation is concerned. In themselves they have no future. These false teachers are like that; they have no future. Peter then says they talk boldly about things of which they are ignorant, and they will perish in the very destruction they are engaged in spreading around. One translation puts it like this: "But these men act by instinct, like wild animals born to be captured and killed; they insult things they do not understand. They will be destroyed like wild animals; they will be paid with suffering for the suffering they caused."

Peter, in speaking about false prophets, does not call them beasts. He says "as brute beasts," meaning they are like that in the sense they act with no consciousness of things. Jesus of Nazareth made a statement like this, "Cast not pearls before swine." He did not say they were swine, but He meant that they acted like swine. If you threw pearls in front of swine, they would trample the pearls underfoot because they would not want to eat pearls; they want to eat barley, and the pearls would not be appreciated. That was the point Jesus was making, and this is the point Peter is making here. False prophets were acting like animals in that they had no appreciation of anything more than their natural instincts.

Another translation puts it this way: "These men are like brute beasts, born in the course of nature to be caught and

killed. They pour abuse upon things they do not understand;
like the beasts they will perish, suffering hurt for the hurt they
have inflicted."

All of this is being said about people who set themselves up
as teachers right among the believers, having one characteris-
tic in common: they belittle spiritual things. The believer
should be very careful about anybody who talks loosely and
carelessly about heaven and the things of God.

THE ARROGANCE OF FALSE TEACHERS
(2 Peter 2:13)

Have you ever noticed how some persons can and will stay
with a group long after they have no interest in what that group
is doing?

> And shall receive the reward of unrighteousness, as they that
> count it pleasure to riot in the daytime. Spots they are and
> blemishes, sporting themselves with their own deceivings while
> they feast with you (2 Peter 2:13).

Believers in Christ living here on earth certainly do not
know everything about heaven and about God. They need to
learn, so teachers are necessary. In the early days, from the
time Israel came out of the land of Egypt, they needed Moses
to lead them; after that they had Joshua. From time to time
they fell into bondage and it took a man like Gideon to lead
them to freedom. In the New Testament, Jesus of Nazareth,
Himself a Master Teacher, was followed by the apostles who
were sent forth to teach. Believers in Christ learn from others.
This is where Peter issued his warning, because certain leaders
are not sound or true in their leadership. Some who mislead
may not understand what they are doing: they are doing it in
ignorance. They may even be well meaning people and God
may graciously overrule them in their ignorance; but that is not
true in every case. There are others who pose a much more
sinister threat. They are the ones Peter was talking about. They
are the ones who do not believe that Jesus Christ was born of a
virgin, or that He performed miracles. Nor do they believe in

the literal resurrection for the dead or in the Ascension. Many may be in the pulpit, or teaching a Bible class.

Speaking of these false teachers, Peter wrote, "And they shall receive the reward of unrighteousness, as they that count it pleasure to riot in the daytime." What is the reward of unrighteousness? Does that not remind us of Paul, who speaks about the wages of sin being death? Death is not only the end; death begins with degeneration. If you say that a person counts it pleasure to riot in the daytime, you would mean that he openly flaunts his deviation from the truth. Some people openly make a show of the fact they are not like the narrow-minded "fanatics" of a by-gone generation.

Peter then wrote, "Spots they are and blemishes." They are a spot on whom? They are a spot on the believers in Christ, and a blemish on the believer. They are a blot upon the record of believers. Every now and again we find a congregation that elects a man to the position of teacher of the men's Bible class who does not even believe the Bible; yet he is there teaching the men's Bible class! "Sporting themselves with their own deceivings while they feast with you." Here is a sobering thought: they seem to be entirely at ease with their own views. They enjoy the discomfort they spread.

Some years ago when I was a professor at a seminary I was asked to conduct Bible classes in the evenings as a service to the students, because some students wanted more attention given to the Scriptures. There were other students who actually made sneering remarks about "bedtime stories." These students were at ease with their views, yet they were quite deceived in their own errors, and they were allowed to stay in the seminary. Such persons depend on the believer in Christ being so polite that they will never be asked any questions. Often a person is frowned upon if he raises a question about anyone teaching who is not telling the truth. Peter said to the believers in Christ: "Be careful; beware."

THE EVIL INFLUENCE OF FALSE TEACHERS
(2 Peter 2:14)

Have you ever noticed that when a person is unwilling to obey God his influence upon others is all bad?

> Having eyes full of adultery, and that cannot cease from sin; beguiling unstable souls: a heart they have exercised with covetous practices; cursed children (2 Peter 2:14).

When is a person a true believer? There is far more involved than ideas. A person is not a believer in Christ because he has the same ideas that you have. Involved in being a true believer is a personal relationship with Jesus Christ. It is not a case of a person who says what I say, or who even thinks along the line that I think; but a person who lives as I seek to live in the Lord. Such a person obeys the Lord; he trusts Him and he decides what he will do according to the Word of God; he follows after values that have been set forth by the Lord. That is the kind of person who is trustworthy.

One cannot always tell who is reliable by looking. One has to be careful about such things. Paul said, "If any man love not the Lord Jesus Christ, let him be Anathema" (1 Cor. 16:22), meaning let him be accursed. Many people have shied away from that statement as if Paul had been too harsh. But if one is associating with anybody who is writing or speaking and is not seeking the glory of the living Lord Jesus Christ as a matter of procedure, one should avoid that person. Do not the Scriptures say, "How can two walk together except they be agreed?"

Peter continues his warning about people who would lead believers in Christ astray; and in this 14th verse he says four things about them. The first one is, "Having eyes full of adultery, and that cannot cease from sin." The most common understanding of adultery is that it is a matter of an immoral relationship between a man and a woman. What can often be missed is that the Bible uses this term to indicate an inferior, or a wrong worship. Adultery is spoken of in the Old Testament about people who turned away from the worship of Jehovah to worship Baal and Ashtaroth, or who worshiped the gods of Babylon and Assyria.

James put it this way:

Ye adulterers and adulteresses, know ye not that the friendship
of the world is enmity with God? whosoever therefore will be a
friend of the world is the enemy of God (James 4:4).

That is what Peter is talking about, something in the heart,
where the affection of the heart has been given to someone or
something else. This is the significance of the word "adultery."
Spiritually speaking, the word "adultery" implies becoming
interested in someone other than God and in something other
than the truth. James uses that thought, and he and Peter seem
to have very much the same frame of mind.

"Having eyes full of adultery" can include very properly the
idea that these teachers have their minds full of things other
than that found in the Bible; they accept other views. They
know the Bible teaches certain things, but they read other
authors. When the Scripture says, "That cannot cease from
sin," it can be they cannot cease from being selfish and following their own ideas. It is sin when we do what we want to do,
and not what God wants us to do. Think about that in this
connection. Perhaps they fell into the practice of physical
adultery and other ordinary practices of sin, but I think Peter is
dealing with something broader than that.

The next thing is that the false teacher is "beguiling unstable
souls." Who would be an unstable soul? This would mean a
person who is not settled. In Ephesians 4:14 Paul speaks about
children tossed to and fro with every wind of doctrine. Children are immature people. "A heart they have exercised with
covetous practices." This does not refer only to money; it will
include anything I want. Finally Peter names them, "cursed
children." Who would they be? People who do not love the
Lord Jesus Christ are cursed (1 Cor. 16:22). People who preach
error as Paul spoke of these in Galatia ought to be cursed (Gal.
1:8-9). And people who are willful in sin, like the man we read
about in chapter 5 of First Corinthians would be cursed of God.
These are the people and this is the description of those who
would, by their teaching, lead men astray. Thus Peter warns
believers in Christ to be careful about listening to and following
anyone who brings a different message than what they have
heard and believed.

SOME TEACHERS ARE LED ASTRAY
(2 Peter 2:15-16)

Can you believe that a person could begin serving the Lord and then change his loyalty?

> Which have forsaken the right way, and are gone astray, following the way of Balaam the son of Bosor, who loved the wages of unrighteousness; but was rebuked for his iniquity: the dumb ass speaking with man's voice forbad the madness of the prophet (2 Peter 2:15-16).

This is a fearful thought. It is terrible to think that a person could start out walking with the Lord, then begin walking in another direction. But the man Judas Iscariot is an example of this. How could he associate with Jesus of Nazareth for perhaps three years, ministering in His name, enjoying fellowship with the other apostles, and then betray his Lord? Apparently because a man starts walking with the Lord is no guarantee that he will keep it up. I wish it were different. It would be wonderful if we could be sure that when a person has said he would, then for sure he would, but this does not follow. Sometimes a person starts to serve and then gradually veers away and begins serving elsewhere.

In writing about various people associated with him, Paul speaks of a certain man whom he called Demas, saying to Timothy, "Demas hath forsaken me, having loved this present world" (2 Tim. 4:10). He refers to others with the comment, "They went out from us." And in one place he said in effect: "No doubt they needed to go out from us because they did not believe like we did any more and it needed to become clear that they belonged to a different crowd of people."

This is an unhappy line of thought, but I suspect that which has to do with keeping anything clean is never very pleasant; from the time a boy gets his face scrubbed, until the time when a woman tries to keep the floors clean, or a man tries to keep the car clean. It is a fact that constant loyalty cannot be assumed; one cannot be sure about it. Perhaps the most dangerous persons are those who started with sincere spiritual experience and gradually changed to become something else.

The classic case of this in the Bible is the prophet Balaam, and Peter refers to him in the passage we have before us now. This was an Old Testament incident which is significant for us.

Peter is speaking about false teachers and here he described them like this, "Which have forsaken the right way, and are gone astray (apparently they had started out right but they forsook the right way), following the way of Balaam the son of Bosor, who loved the wages of unrighteousness; but was rebuked for his iniquity: the dumb ass speaking with man's voice forbad the madness of the prophet." This incident is recorded in Numbers 22, where verse 5 begins the story of this prophet, Balaam. Briefly, a king by the name of Balak wanted help from some spiritual power to resist the oncoming people of Israel. He sent for Balaam, who had power, and asked him to curse Israel. At first Balaam said he could not curse Israel, but when he was promised riches, he went along with Balak.

The amazing thing is that Balaam tried to tell the truth, even though he was in the service of a man who was opposed to it. Balaam had had dealings with God, and he believed in God in the sense that he believed God was holy and all powerful; but for personal advantage he was willing to go along with a man opposed to God's people. This is the case of a man who really wanted to do the will of God finding himself collaborating with people who did not want to do the will of God. Why? For money.

What tempts a man like that, and what can tempt a preacher, is not always money. Sometimes a man is tempted by prestige. He is promised that if he will make certain compromises he will be acceptable and obtain a better position. Some people will actually make something of politics out of it. They will remain quiet when they should not, or they will endorse certain things, maneuvering and manipulating things with an eye to an advantage they are getting. This is what Balaam did.

I am primarily interested here in the warning Peter gave. Actually the whole situation of leadership among believers in Christ is really not so complicated today as it may seem. Ask the leaders a few questions. First of all, about the Scripture itself. What about the authority of the Scriptures, the integrity of the Bible? Do you think the Bible is the Word of God, or don't you? Leaders can be separated right at that point. What about the things of the Lord Jesus Christ; do you think the Gospel stories are real? Do you think Jesus Christ is living today, and that He is at the right hand of God, praying for you?

Some think so; these are one group, the true leaders. Others do not think so; they are a different group, the false teachers. Do you think Christ is coming again in clouds from heaven in great glory? All is really quite simple; do you really believe in the Lord Jesus Christ? Then follow Him. If you do not really believe in Him, in spite of anything you say or in spite of any church you attend, if you do not really follow the Lord Jesus Christ, you do not belong. That is what Peter would say.

FALSE TEACHERS ARE BARREN
(2 Peter 2:17)

Do you realize that the faith of a believer in Christ must be real?

> These are wells without water, clouds that are carried with a tempest; to whom the mist of darkness is reserved for ever (2 Peter 2:17).

One of the greatest pitfalls that hinder blessing in spiritual experience is to allow faith to remain a matter of opinion, or just a matter of what we think or say. To be sure it is important to witness to one's faith by words. The Scriptures say, "Let the redeemed of the Lord say so." But it is even more important to act in line with one's word, or in line with the promises of God. We know it is true that actions speak louder than words, and this is especially true in matters of faith. In the Bible we find that again and again there have been those who said they believed but who did not. Sad to say these were to be found right among the Lord's people.

Jesus of Nazareth told the parable of the wheat and the tares. The tares were weeds growing in the midst of the wheat. So it is with reference to believers. In one of the parables Jesus told of a fisherman who threw a net into the sea and took in all manner of fish; some good and some bad. This is the way it is with believers. There are real believers, but there are some who are not real. Those who are not real do not bear fruit. "They say but they do not." Such persons talk as if they were believers in Christ, but they do not walk as if they were really believers in Christ. Peter warns that one of the characteristics of false teaching is that it does not produce results.

John pressed this point in First John 3:18, "Let us not love in word, neither in tongue; but in deed and in truth." James discussed it at length in James 2:14-26. "What doth it profit, my brethren, though a man say he hath faith, and have not works? can faith save him?" After he has discussed this problem, James wrote, "Faith, if it hath not works, is dead, being alone." This is what Peter brought out: the public may not know for sure just what a man actually is in his heart, and they may not know for sure how a man is actually related to the Lord Jesus Christ; but they are always skeptical of those who talk much when they walk little. This sort of conduct affects people.

Peter pointed out that this is a trait of false teachers, "These are wells without water, clouds that are carried with a tempest; to whom the mist of darkness is reserved for ever." This described something that is inept; that does not amount to anything. Another version says they are like dried-up springs, and another that they are springs that give no water, while one translation says, "Wells without a drop of water in them." They have the appearance but none of the results. The poet Milton wrote this of conditions in the church of his day, "The hungry sheep look up and are not fed."

When no spiritual benefit is derived from a church service and everybody's heart is left cold, something is wrong. Peter speaks of "clouds that are carried with a tempest." Have you ever watched clouds in a storm? They may look big and dark, but they do not provide rain. One translator speaks of "the changing shape of whirling storm clouds." Such clouds are impressive but they do not amount to anything. In my boyhood days at certain seasons of the year rain was very desirable on the farm; and it was discouraging when a certain kind of cloud came up, because it would not give rain. We would say about them, "All wind and no rain." That is the way it is with false teachers. It is possible to go through all the motions of teaching and all the motions of preaching, and yet have no results.

This was the condition of these leaders about whom Peter was writing. We might think that false teachers would sound wrong, as if there were something untrue in the very words they used. But we shall see in our next study this was not the case at all. As a matter of fact, such persons would probably use ingratiating statements; they would say things that would sound very good and impressive, but there would be no results.

Every now and again a meeting is held with large crowds of people coming and going, but no one really sees results. What kind of results should one expect? One could expect that people would be thinking more about God, turning to Him. Some people would begin to read the Bible, and also some people would set aside certain wrong practices. There would be results if the blessing of God was upon the work; but there would be no blessing if the preacher is not telling the truth as God would have it told. Peter warned there would be no spiritual results when the teaching is false.

DECEIVED THROUGH VANITY
(2 Peter 2:18)

Do you know that people can be influenced by smooth talkers?

> For when they speak great swelling words of vanity they allure through the lusts of the flesh, through much wantonness, those that were clean escaped from them who live in error (2 Peter 2:18).

After Peter had urged the believers to put into action what they really believed in Christ Jesus, he took time to warn them against teachers who would lead them into error. This second chapter is a vivid description of those who would do so. One may wonder how anybody could be led astray by such empty performances as Peter described, but he now pointed out how it is done, "For when they speak great swelling words of vanity" (mind you, they do not advertise it like that; they use big words with a good swing to them and especially will there be words of vanity; not only vanity of their own but they will appeal to our vanity) "they allure through the lusts of the flesh." Now the lusts of the flesh are not necessarily appetites only;

they include pride and personal interest, your ego; the desires
of the flesh. "Through much wantonness, those that were clean
escaped from them who live in error." Although the language
implied a certain type of immorality it did not mean that this
was physical immorality; this is spiritual immorality which
these people exercised. For instance, in another translation we
read, "They make proud and stupid statements." Of course,
they do not advertise that they are stupid. "They make proud
and stupid statements, and use immoral bodily lusts to trap
those who are just beginning to escape from among people who
live in error."

How can anybody escape from people who live in error? If
you believe in the Lord Jesus Christ, receiving Him to be your
Savior, you deny yourself. Just as surely as you deny yourself,
you escape from those who live in error. When living in error
you praise yourself, and when you are proud and self-centered
that is error. If you are to escape from that, one way is to reckon
yourself dead. But it happens that reckoning yourself dead will
not mean that you are absolutely dead; you will actually have
human life in you. This human life can be appealed to and this
is what those folks will do. In still another translation, "They
utter big, empty words, and make of sensual lusts and de-
bauchery a bait to catch those who have barely begun to escape
from their heathen environment."

This is the tragedy; such false teachers will appeal to and win
young believers, persons who are still like children driven by
the wind and tossed about, back and forth. Young believers can
be influenced by the big empty words of those who preach to
make impressive talk and to attract attention. Another translator had a different way of wording it but the idea is the same,
"With their high sounding nonsense they use the sensual pull
of the lower passions to attract those who were just on the point
of cutting loose from their companions in misconduct." And
still another puts it this way, "For uttering loud boasts of folly,
they beguile and lure with lustful desires of the flesh those who
are barely escaping from them who are wrongdoers."

It is difficult to believe that this refers to teachers in spiritual
circles. The language in which it is expressed suggests a somewhat crude immorality, but the situation is that of Sunday
school teaching. We are reminded of the occasion when Jesus

told His disciples that He must go to Jerusalem to die, and how Peter urged Him not to go. Jesus said, "Get thee behind me, Satan." In writing to the Thessalonians, Paul made a point that he did not use flattering words when he was talking to them.

Persons are always susceptible when they are not really dedicated to the Lord; when they are not fully crucified. When they are not crucified the ego is still there, and the ego can be appealed to. When the ego is appealed to, so that the person is thinking in terms of how he will be affected, that is never good. These false teachers are never obvious in what is false, and they are not crude in the way they speak. They are smooth talkers who flatter their hearers by appealing to their ego. Yet this will be effective only when the believers who are listening are immature. But it can happen and this is why Peter warned them. How we need to be faithful to the Lord in our witness and in our testimony!

THE FATAL BLEMISH IN FALSE LEADERS
(2 Peter 2:19)

Do you realize that each of us acts as he is influenced?

> While they promise them liberty, they themselves are the servants of corruption: for of whom a man is overcome, of the same is he brought in bondage (2 Peter 2:19).

Jesus of Nazareth in the Sermon on the Mount made this statement, "Ye cannot serve God and mammon," and we think of that as we look at this verse. In our conduct all of us are actually being influenced. Perhaps some of us feel that we are unattached, that we serve no one, but that is a grave mistake. Those who have heard the Gospel of Christ know that it becomes a bit specific by saying it is either self or Christ. Some who stand around doing nothing think they are acting independently. What they really mean is that they are doing exactly what they want to do, independent of anybody else and independent of God and Christ.

I suspect folks generally do not realize that each person is under the influence of gravitation. The reason why I walk on the ground is because I seem to be pulled down to the ground. In the physical world there seems to be an attraction, a power, between bodies of mass, holding these bodies together as a string would hold two stones together. Apparently this is the force that causes the revolution of the planets around the sun. Almost everybody knows that our planets go around the sun and that they are held in place by this power which we call gravitation.

We get an idea of what this would be like if we take a weight of any kind, a stone, a piece of iron, or a piece of wood, and tie it on a string or rope, and swing it around. What holds that stone there in that circle is the string to which it is tied. That circle is what is meant by an orbit. Actually that weight flies around in a certain orbit, and what determines the orbit is the length of the rope. This truth can be seen in any group of people, when each member has a certain relation to the leader. They are tied to him with certain loyalty or fear and they move around accordingly as they are attached to him.

Something like this is true in the believer in Christ, so that I can use this figure of speech in saying that the believer orbits around Christ. What holds the believer in Christ in place? Let me suggest that the Holy Spirit is the power that draws the believer to Christ, and the Holy Spirit of God is the power that holds believers in orbit, going around with Jesus Christ as the center in their spiritual awareness, their spiritual relationship. In common spiritual experience there are two centers of influence, as there are two planes of operation, commonly called by Paul flesh and spirit. The flesh is a plane in which the believer travels around with the flesh in the center, and he conducts himself according to his own personal estimate of himself. The other plane or field of operation is spirit, and this is centered in Christ.

Many of the words I have used can be eliminated. You could simply think in your mind of flesh on the one hand and spirit on the other. Where there is flesh, you would put in the very center "self"; and where there is spirit you would put in the very center "Christ." Peter has been warning believers against false teachers. Here he draws attention to another aspect of their falseness, "While they promise them liberty, they themselves are the servants of corruption." Here we can feel that Peter is referring to natural processes as they are seen in the flesh. When Peter says, "They promise them liberty," he means liberty from the natural consequences of the natural processes, because when nature works out the way it does, the person will become interested in himself and he will be self-centered, egotistic. This is natural. A person can be free from that, as in the Gospel he is promised liberty from this natural consequence. When false teachers are preaching they will promise people freedom while they are themselves the servants of corruption.

We naturally think of corruption as very disagreeable, as the final stage of degeneration and deterioration. When a thing becomes corrupted it is a whole mess of ugly decayed matter. Corruption is the natural state into which dying leads. Paul says the spirit of man is born in corruption but is raised in the newness of life in incorruption. By the word "corruption" we mean something that is dying all the time, and that is the way with anything that is natural. The Gospel of Christ promises to deliver, to set a person free, from the natural course of events. People who are not free are actually involved in something that is dying all the time. Let me say it this way: the only way to be free really from the flesh is to crucify it. Peter is implying here that false leaders are persons who preach as if they were believers in Christ, but they have never crucified the flesh. They have never put themselves to death; they have never reckoned themselves to be dead indeed unto sin. They are still married to the flesh.

The only way to be free from self is to deny it and to follow Christ. In place of self the believer follows Christ. This is what false leaders do not do. They promise freedom as the Gospel would promise it, but they have not crucified themselves; so they are still the servants of corruption. Peter continues, "For of whom a man is overcome, of the same is he brought in bondage." If I were overcome by the Lord, I would be under Him; but if I am not in Him then I am still in the natural processes, and I am in bondage.

THE SNARE OF FALSE TEACHERS
(2 Peter 2:20)

Have you ever heard that if a person has been sick and starts to get well, then suffers a relapse, his sickness can be worse than it was before?

> For if after they have escaped the pollutions of the world through the knowledge of the Lord and Saviour Jesus Christ, they are again entangled therein, and overcome, the latter end is worse with them than the beginning (2 Peter 2:20).

The apostle Paul wrote to the Galatians, "You did run well, who did hinder you that you should not obey the truth?" He had been in that part of the country and had preached the Gospel; the people had believed and in believing they had been greatly blessed. While Paul was away, someone began to talk to them distracting them, and when Paul heard what had happened he wrote the above message. It is possible to make a good start and to be diverted. Some seem to think that becoming a believer in Christ is something that happens in a moment and is then taken for granted. In a sense becoming a believer in Christ is something that is like getting married. It is just the commencement. I know of no way a young couple can more quickly get into trouble than to assume that because they had a wedding they can afford to neglect each other and ignore the responsibilities of being married.

Being a believer in Christ is somewhat like being born. Let us look at this more closely. Has it ever occurred to you that a mother who gives birth to a baby is much busier after the baby is born than she was before? The notion that becoming a believer in Christ is the end is an error. There is an aspect of truth in it; something very definite does happen when we accept Christ: we begin walking with God. And so we say that salvation begins in a crisis, but it goes on in a process. Accepting Jesus Christ is not something you do standing still. While you may accept Christ sitting in a church, spiritually speaking you are starting on something. There is a great promise of deliverance from the flesh, because when you start walking with the Lord you get away chiefly from yourself.

This is why Peter wrote this second epistle; he wanted the

believers to go on through into the newness of life that is in Christ Jesus, the hope of glory. But the word "Christ" is more than just a name, this means the functioning of the living Lord Himself operating in the believer by His Holy Spirit, and that is the hope of glory for the believer. This is the only thing in the believer that will give any assurance that glory will actually be attained. It is a process. When the believer starts walking with Christ he is going some place; he will not need to hunt where to go; Christ will lead him. But he will leave something behind: the things of self.

Now Peter, wanting the believers in Christ to reach up into the precious promises of God, knows that there are false teachers who stop short of following through into the newness of life. "For if after they have escaped the pollutions of the world through the knowledge of the Lord and Saviour Jesus Christ, they are again entangled therein, and overcome, the latter end is worse with them than the beginning." There is nothing inspiring about a mud hole, and that is what this is. There is nothing inspiring about a sore that gets worse and worse, and that is what this does. Believers should recognize this, and Peter is saying that if they really want the blessing of God they must persevere, but they must also be careful.

At this point he is speaking negatively (but still, what he says is true): believers in Christ must avoid listening to people who do not go through into the liberty that is in Christ Jesus. He says, "They are worse than if they were people of the world." It is far better to listen to a man who makes no profession of faith, than it is to listen to a man who claims to be a believer in Christ but is not honoring the Lord Jesus Christ. This is tremendously important. Jesus of Nazareth said,

> When the unclean spirit is gone out of a man, he walketh through dry places, seeking rest, and findeth none. Then he saith, I will return into my house from whence I came out; and when he is come, he findeth it empty, swept, and garnished. Then goeth he, and taketh with himself seven other spirits more wicked than himself, and they enter in and dwell there: and the last state of that man is worse than the first. Even so shall it be also unto this wicked generation (Matt. 12:43-45).

Failing to move on into the newness of life will leave a person in the flesh. These false teachers talked about the benefits of the Gospel, but they walked in themselves, in their own strength. They would talk about what it meant to be a believer in Christ but they lived the way they wanted to live, and thought the things they wanted to think. Peter said if they turned to Christ in the beginning and really wanted to follow Him, and then settled for less and began to follow their own ways, those people would be worse afterwards. What Peter is particularly anxious about is that believers in Christ should not listen to them when they teach.

To sum up: all Peter meant about these false teachers is that they did not follow through in faith into the newness of life that is in Christ Jesus. Believers in Christ should not listen to them because Peter wanted them to become fruitful. He wanted them to become really committed to God and to the Lord Jesus Christ; this can follow if they walk with Him.

THE SAD PLIGHT OF THOSE WHO TURN BACK
(2 Peter 2:21-22)

Do you realize that it is possible for a person to live a professing spiritual life for a while, and then return to worldliness even worse than before?

> For it had been better for them not to have known the way of righteousness, than, after they have known it, to turn from the holy commandment delivered unto them. But it is happened unto them according to the true proverb, The dog is turned to his own vomit again; and the sow that was washed to her wallowing in the mire (2 Peter 2:21-22).

Let me remind you that Peter wrote to believers in Christ. He wanted them to continue believing in Jesus Christ until they had their fruit in holiness. The world probably understands the call of the Gospel, perhaps because it is clearly applicable to the world. We preach the Gospel by showing that if sinners stay where they are, they will be destroyed; if they come to the Lord Jesus Christ they will be saved. This is wonderful and it can be powerful. We thank God for every blessing this message brings.

Now the world not only knows the evangelistic message but

the world can also see the relapses. They can see the failures, whom they call hypocrites. It is common then for the world to make a very simple mistake; they blame the Gospel for the failure. That is like blaming the soil because you have no garden. If you do not plant the garden and cultivate it, you will have no garden. There is no way to stop the people in the world from making this mistake, because they do not know better. When persons professing faith fail to follow the Lord, and act like hypocrites, they bring the Gospel into reproach. Becoming a believer in Christ is something I do that is caused by God. But He does not do this arbitrarily. God calls and, for every one who comes, God works in him to will and to do of His good pleasure. In response to faith, God works in grace; accepting Jesus Christ is not only accepting Him as Savior but as Lord. When a person accepts Jesus Christ he accepts the Lord Jesus as Savior from sin. He accepts Christ into the newness of life. It is a matter of committing self to follow the Lord Jesus Christ and to obey Him.

Warning against stopping short is often expressed in the Bible very bluntly. Some expressions in the Bible are distasteful but it is the way the Bible makes the idea effective. We are told in the Book of Revelation that the Lord Jesus sent word to the church of Laodicea that because they were lukewarm He would spew them out of His mouth, meaning He will spit them out.

Two animals are spoken of in Scripture referring to different aspects of spiritual experience. They are found on almost all farms. The one we commonly speak about is sheep, and the other that we seldom speak about is swine, or hogs. In the attitude these animals have toward mud we see a basic difference in people. A sheep does many foolish things, but it hates the mud. The Lord Jesus is the Good Shepherd; when anyone really hates sin and does not want to do wrong, he has the sheep attitude. We tell a person like that the Lord Jesus Christ is a good Shepherd. But the Bible has several things to say about swine; one is that we should not cast our pearls before swine. Thus it speaks about people who do not appreciate spiritual things. Here, in Peter, it is a matter of loving and wallowing in the mud.

In this passage Peter warned about this, "The dog is turned

to his own vomit again; and the sow that was washed to her wallowing in the mire." The modern translations state it differently, one puts it this way, "It would have been much better for them never to have known the way of righteousness than to know it and then turn away from the sacred command that was given them." Another reads thus: "How much better never to have known the right way than, having known it, to turn back and abandon the sacred commandments delivered to them! For them the proverb has proved true: 'The dog returns to its own vomit, and the sow after a wash rolls in the mud again.' " Still another expressed it thus: "It would be better for them not to have known the way of goodness at all rather than after knowing it to turn their backs on the sacred commandments given to them. Alas, for them the old proverbs have come true about the dog returning to his vomit and the sow that had been washed going back to wallow in the muck."

Should we not preach the Gospel because some will be like that? That is like saying we should never ride in a car because some people drive too fast. May the Lord keep us true to Him.

SECOND PETER
Chapter 3

✝   ✝   ✝

STIRRED UP BY REMEMBERING SCRIPTURE
(2 Peter 3:1-2)

Do you realize that to arouse the spiritual consciousness of a person you should remind him of what he has heard about God?

> This second epistle, beloved, I now write unto you; in both which I stir up your pure minds by way of remembrance: that ye may be mindful of the words which were spoken before by the holy prophets, and of the commandment of us the apostles of the Lord and Saviour (2 Peter 3:1-2).

Human beings think about things in which they are interested. Appetite or hunger arouses interest. For example, a person who is hungry will be interested in food. A person who has time on his hands will be interested in amusement; a person who is cold will be interested in getting warm; and a person who is lonely will be interested in friends.

It is not natural for a human being to think about God, because he has not seen God; he has not experienced God person to person. It is not natural to think about heaven or about the soul, or any one of these spiritual things which are invisible. Left to himself, a man probably would not ever think about the God of the Bible. Now mind you, he could be lonely, and he could be weak and in trouble, but he would not think about the God of the Bible, because he would not know about Him.

The ordinary mind of the natural man is not what Peter here would call pure (unselfish). The mind of man is selfish and he is very likely to be thinking about things that concern himself:

what is for him; what he can do. But the regenerated man, who has new life, is conscious of God and of Christ. He is conscious of heaven, of the soul and eternity; and this consciousness is kept in him by the Holy Spirit of God. The regenerated man has a spiritual mind, and this is what Peter means when he speaks of a pure mind or a purified man. When we read, "This second epistle, beloved, I now write unto you; in both which I stir up your pure minds by way of remembrance," we should remember their minds were pure, not because they had never done wrong, or were always what they ought to be. The only way the mind of any human being can be pure is when it has been made pure by the grace of God. So these minds have been purified in the sense that the selfishness has been taken out of them, because they have been born again. Their interest is now in Christ Jesus and not in self.

These pure minds were stirred up, made to come alive as it were, and become active, stimulated to action by way of remembrance. Any spiritual person has both kinds of minds: a human mind because he has a human body and he grew up as a human being, and a spiritual mind wherein he is conscious of the things of God. Since Christ is in him, so the mind of Christ can be in him. A believer in Christ has a new man inside as well as the old man.

When Peter wanted to share some spiritual truths he endeavored to arouse the spiritual mind. He did this by reminding the people of the revelation from God, "I stir up your pure minds by way of remembrance: that ye may be mindful of the words which were spoken before by the holy prophets, and of the commandment of us the apostles of the Lord and Saviour." It is the words of the prophets and of the apostles that will keep the minds stirred up, spiritually speaking. Let me remind you again: anybody who is a believer in Christ has been made conscious of the fact that God has revealed His will. God has revealed things in Christ Jesus that we never would have known had it not been for Him. This is revealed in the Living Word, the Lord Jesus Christ, and in the written Word, the Bible.

Peter said stern things about those who have wrong ideas; he said harsh things about false prophets, but he wanted believers in Christ to know they are beloved. He would not have written about these things if he had not cared for the believers, and they were not to lose sight of this fact. "I stir up your pure minds by way of remembrance" (reminding them of the transfiguration) "of the words which were spoken before by the holy prophets, and of the commandment of us the apostles of the Lord and Saviour." Nobody will ever understand the things of God naturally, even a believer in Christ. If you started talking to me about the things that God is going to do, I would not be able to understand you unless I remembered the things that had been revealed about God. I need to remember the living God; I need to remember the promises of God: I need to remember the things God has said and done in the course of the history of His people. Then I will be able to understand what you are saying to me now. When Peter wrote, "that ye may be mindful," he meant that they might give full attention to the words spoken by the holy prophets, which, generally speaking, could by expressed in one word: repent.

In order to be saved of God a person must really mean it when he comes to worship Him. The prophets repeated this over and over. The prophets did not have to put together the ceremony of worship in the tabernacle and in the temple; Aaron did that. The prophets told the people that just repeating the Ten Commandments and going through the motions of the tabernacle was not enough. The prophets preached repentance. The commandment of the Lord and Savior is: believe and be saved. In other words, man should be conscious that God has called, as in the Old Testament times; and He has promised, as in the New Testament times. If you know these things you can benefit by what Peter will tell you in the rest of this third chapter of Second Peter.

SOME RIDICULE CHRIST'S RETURN
(2 Peter 3:3-4)

How should we feel about anyone who ridicules the idea of the end of the world?

Knowing this first, that there shall come in the last days scoffers, walking after their own lusts, and saying, Where is the promise of his coming? for since the fathers fell asleep, all things continue as they were from the beginning of the creation (2 Peter 3:3-4).

What we have here is based upon the event promised in Acts 1:11, "This same Jesus, which is taken up from you into heaven, shall so come in like manner as ye have seen him go into heaven." Jesus of Nazareth ascended in full view of all, and this is the manner in which He will come again. Remember this also: it was a company of His own believers who saw Him go. They were gathered together to worship Him and they witnessed His going. A cloud received Him out of their sight. We read in Second Thessalonians that He will come in the clouds of heaven and in great glory.

Many believers in Christ have developed various ideas about His coming again. We have heard all manner of different suggestions, some of them very specific, carefully worked out, telling us exactly when and what He will do; but the gist of all is clear that He will come back. As a student I preached at a church in Winnipeg, and I felt it was my responsibility to give a well-rounded presentation of the Gospel truths. A preacher cannot tell all he knows each Sunday, so many of us in our preaching tend to have a one-sided emphasis: the one we are thinking about at the time. In order to present a balanced emphasis I decided I would preach on various subjects according to the proportion that these were presented in the Bible. The time came when I felt I should preach about the return of the Lord. I preached an outline something like this: He was raised from the dead, and I talked about the resurrection. He went up into heaven, and I talked about the ascension. He is coming like that again. When it was over a member of my congregation came to me greatly disturbed. She took me to task for preaching in that manner from the pulpit. She was shocked to hear a preacher say the Lord is coming back. But that is what the Scriptures say and I felt I should preach it.

The greatest hindrance, apparently, to preaching and teaching the coming of the Lord is fear of ridicule. The reason the coming again of the Lord seems so easily ridiculed is that much of it is unseen. If you believe in the return of the Lord Jesus Christ, you will have to believe other related things. You will have to believe in the reality of God and of heaven. You will have to believe in the reality of spiritual things, in the reality of the resurrection and of the ascension, and in the reality of the authority of the revelation of God in His Word. Many people cannot believe the message.

In chapter 3 Peter writes, "Knowing this first, that there shall come in the last days scoffers, walking after their own lusts, and saying, Where is the promise of his coming? for since the fathers fell asleep, all things continue as they were from the beginning of the creation." Isn't that interesting? At the beginning of the Christian church there were people making fun of the idea of the Lord coming back. Peter pointed out that scoffers shall come in the last days, walking according to their desires. Their consciousness moves along the lines of their own wishes.

In my opinion the last days in God's overall program are the days between the ascension of the Lord Jesus Christ and His coming again. Humans lived on the earth a long time before Christ came. The prophets told them of the coming of the Lord Jesus Christ, the Son of God, the Messiah. He lived here a short time. After He was put to death He was raised from the dead. His last outward public event was His ascension into heaven. The next event in God's program is the return of the Lord Jesus Christ. He is now praying for us. So He is to come back, and I think the "last days" are between the time He went up and the time He is coming back. "There shall come in the last days scoffers." Here the important thing for us to remember is that to be forewarned is to be forearmed.

OLD WORLD DESTROYED BY WATER
(2 Peter 3:5-6)

Do you realize that for anybody to be ignorant of the creation story, he must *want* to be ignorant about it?

> For this they willingly are ignorant of, that by the word of God the heavens were of old, and the earth standing out of the water and in the water: whereby the world that then was, being overflowed with water, perished (2 Peter 3:5-6).

In the beginning God created the heavens and the earth. This statement is so plain any teacher of the ways of God must know about it. Peter talks about teachers, and while we realize many people in the world do not know what is in the Bible, a teacher of the Christian Gospel should know what is in it. So Peter is saying that no matter what their particular attitude may be, all teachers of the Gospel should know the plain and simple truth that in the beginning God created the heavens and the earth. Anyone remaining ignorant of the simple Genesis account of creation wanted to be ignorant.

I now draw your attention to something in our last study: the people who ridiculed the coming of the Lord say there is no evidence in nature about His coming. They said, "Where is the promise of his coming? for since the fathers fell asleep, all things continue as they were from the beginning of the creation." In other words, all of the natural processes continue unabated, and for that reason the Lord Jesus will not come because there is no evidence of His coming. Peter presses them hard here; he says it suits their personal human interest to focus attention on nature; they do not want to think about the coming of the Lord Jesus Christ.

Have you ever thought about this: when one of your loved ones died, was there any change in the outside world? Was there change in the shining of the sun, in the blowing of the wind, and did the flowers act differently? Death took place, but the natural processes went on. Even if there is no evidence in nature to show the coming of the Lord, that does not mean that He will not come. Peter says, "This they willingly are ignorant of, that by the word of God the heavens were of old, and the earth standing out of the water and in the water."

John presents the idea that the controlling factor in the work of creation was the Word of God. "In the beginning was the Word, and the Word was with God, and the Word was God" (John 1:1). He then tells us that all things were made by Him and without Him was not anything made that was made. In Hebrews we read, "Through faith we understand that the worlds were framed by the word of God" (Heb. 11:3).

The word of man is his expressed mind, his deliberate intention and his total will. When a man gives you his word he tells you what he is going to do. It is a definite utterance with commitment that he will back up. This is what God wanted to do, to create the world; and so by the Word of God, in the will of God and the expressed intention of God, the whole created world is just the way it is. Peter incorporated the Genesis account as he wrote about the end of the world, because the same Bible that tells us how the world began is the Bible that tells us how the world will end. This is what Peter brought out; the same God who made it is the God who will destroy it. We read, "That by the word of God the heavens were of old, and the earth standing out of the water and in the water: whereby the world that then was, being overflowed with water, perished."

Many of us are inclined to think the word "world" includes heaven and earth, but it is not necessarily so. The word "world" refers rather to the structure in which life takes place, in which living goes on.

When you speak about "world" you are speaking about heaven and earth, it is true; and you are speaking about the soil, the earth, people, and time. The whole living situation is involved, and everything perished. Does this mean that water covered the whole globe? It is not necessarily that way. It does mean the water covered the whole land where people were, and the whole inhabited world was destroyed with water. So let me reiterate: the world was overflowed with water and perished, but the word "world" does not refer to the heavens, as the heavens were not overflowed with water. I mention this because the next verse speaks about the judgment of the heavens, and the earth being judged by fire, and destroyed.

PRESENT WORLD DESTROYED BY FIRE
(2 Peter 3:7)

Do you realize that the Bible says the heavens and the earth as made in creation will be destroyed by fire?

> But the heavens and the earth, which are now, by the same word are kept in store, reserved unto fire against the day of judgment and perdition of ungodly men (2 Peter 3:7).

These words do not mean anything to the natural person. This is Bible language and refers to the created universe. The word "heavens" covers all the starry hosts, everything that we see, the heavens and the earth which now "by the same word are kept in store." Which word? The word that is in verse 5, "By the word of God the heavens were of old, and the earth standing out of the water and in the water," the Word referred to in the first chapter of Genesis, the same Word that actually functioned in creation.

Now we may find it hard to accept the statement that the heavens and the earth are kept by the Word of God. Why do we find that so hard? Is it because we have already accepted other ideas? Do we have something in our mind about the processes of gravitation and about the cosmic powers that move the stars through their courses and keep the planets in their own orbits? Is it because we have a smattering of astronomy in our thinking, and we get to know about these so-called scientific ways of talking about things so that it is hard for us to realize there is a Person back of the whole thing? Is it because in the common talk about the world people are so secular they deal with the world in a material way? Or is it because the common mind leaves out the idea of a personal God? Do we look at the world as if we were looking a machine, but we never think of the Mechanic? If we were to look at the operation of a big factory and see how it is run, nobody is pushing the wheels, we just get the impression that it is a thing of itself without being aware of the fact that a man designed it, and a man put it together and made it go.

You can talk about the world as it goes on in the natural processes, and the first thing you know you are not thinking about how it came into being or about what will happen. You just think about what is going on. You think about the natural processes and they continue over and over. There is morning, noon, and night. There is springtime, summer, harvest, and winter. Then you look at the natural processes and all the different things that happen, the things that happen in the powers that are operative in the physical world and in the electrical world. You become so occupied with all of the various forces that you forget that these things are being held in the hand of Almighty God.

That is the great truth the Bible tells us about the world. Someone may say he likes the processes of nature, they are so exact. Why are they so precise; why does nature act so consistently all the time? These things are held in place by the righteousness of God, and the power that is in the world is a power that comes from the Creator. God not only made it but God keeps it. "The heavens and the earth, which are now, by the same word are kept in store." What word? The Word that created them; the Word that formed them. The same God who created them is the God who is keeping them, reserved unto fire.

This brings to mind that judgment in the Bible is brought out in two different events: by water and by fire. The judgment by water was the flood. The judgment by fire has been promised. That is the end of the world, and this is what Peter is talking about. God made the world; God keeps the world; God will end the world. "Reserved unto fire."

Both these elements, water and fire, have a cleansing effect. We use water to wash away filth, and we use fire to burn out anything that is unclean. Fire is much more drastic than water. Water will wash off what is on the outside, but fire will penetrate all the way through. This would indicate that the first judgment by water was relatively superficial; the second judgment by fire will be thorough and complete, "against the day of judgment and perdition of ungodly men."

Here again we have language that the average man in the street would not begin to think about: the day of judgment. When we speak about that day we are not necessarily limiting it to twenty-four hours. It is the time. The word "day" is used in the Bible about the way we use it in our own language. We speak of a man in the day of his youth; we do not mean one twenty-four-hour period, we mean the time of his youth. The day of his old age is the time of his old age. The day when our children were young embraced several years, and the day when I went to school took several years. The word "day" just means "time."

The day of judgment! Now this word "judgment" is a Bible word. It refers to the judgment that is to come upon the whole world. God will judge the world. The Scripture goes on to say, "And perdition of ungodly men." Saying "of judgment and perdition," does not mean that perdition and judgment are the same. The day of judgment is one concept and perdition of ungodly men is another. On the day of judgment all men will come to be judged, and ungodly men will be doomed; perdition of ungodly refers to their doom. Apparently fire will be involved. It would be well to read the rest of this chapter and remember to pray about these matters. We are not thinking about earthly things; we are thinking about spiritual things. We need help to believe.

NO TIME SCHEDULE WITH GOD
(2 Peter 3:8-9)

Have you ever thought about the fact that God does not act on a time schedule?

> But, beloved, be not ignorant of this one thing, that one day is with the Lord as a thousand years, and a thousand years as one day. The Lord is not slack concerning his promise, as some men count slackness; but is long-suffering to us-ward, not willing that any should perish, but that all should come to repentance (2 Peter 3:8-9).

Time belongs to this world. Men use it and men go by it but it is important to remember that God makes time. If He wants more time He makes more time. Verses 7 and 8 contain a remarkable statement, with two major ideas. The first concerns the subject of time as a whole; the coming again of the Lord Jesus Christ being of special interest. In my judgment this is not generally accepted as a meaningful idea. This is not strange when we consider that people do not want to think even of their own death. Why look ahead to when they will be nothing? A believer would do well to heed the prayer of the psalmist, "So teach us to number our days, that we may apply our hearts unto wisdom" (Ps. 90:12).

How do you feel about the thoughts that are expressed in Second Peter? Do you feel that the subject is not really vital? Do you think, perhaps, that talking about the coming of the

Lord is beside the point? Such an opinion is a reflection of the common unbelief in which we live. Many people do not believe that God is sovereign and that everything is under His hand; that God is Judge and every person will face Him; that God is alive and you can have dealings with Him; that God has a plan and He is going to work things out. Not many people actually believe that heaven is real, just as real as the city in which we live, and is eternal. Heaven is everlasting, never grows old, nor does it come and go. It is far more important than earth. When a person dies, the believer in Christ says that person is better off; this means that he is in a better place. Few of the people we deal with think that Jesus Christ is alive. They may believe He once lived and they know that He was crucified, but not many believe He is now alive, that He has a real body, and that He is in heaven, praying for us.

If you do believe these things, talking about the end of the world is not empty talk. How many people are willing to believe that the Bible teaches the destruction of this world? We look around and see the plants and the birds, the sunset and the sunrise; and then we see the works of men, the big cities, works of art and music. It is incredible that these things will come to an end. It does not seem real. People feel there is really nothing to the coming of the Lord or the end of the world because so much time has passed with no indication of what will happen. Peter wrote these verses long ago, "Beloved, be not ignorant of this one thing, that one day is with the Lord as a thousand years, and a thousand years as one day."

It has been almost 2,000 years since Jesus Christ was here. You could say that is almost like two days. Perhaps you may say, "I have another day to live." In God's sight that is like a thousand years. Now you can understand the simple, sweeping statement in verse 8, a statement that nullifies all time schedules. If you are inclined to figure how long: don't. Someone may ask if I think time is almost finished. I do not know; that is in God's hands. We are warned not to try to estimate the time. The wonderful statement in verse 9 tells us the reason God has not brought judgment to bear: He wants to give as many people as will possibly turn to the Lord an opportunity to do so. This is the gracious reason for the long delay.

No doubt many things in the world bother the Lord, too;

many things that are happening are disagreeable to Him. He is patient. Why? Because He thinks time will change the world? God is dealing with generation after generation, and we could become misled into thinking about the world going on all the time. The world is going on considerably, but men are not going on. God is not willing that any should perish, but that all should come to repentance. Some will perish but it is not what God wants. Our hearts are humbled that Almighty God is actually watching over us, waiting for people to turn to Him.

THE COMING OF THE DAY OF THE LORD
(2 Peter 3:10)

Do you know that the end of the world has been described in the Bible?

> But the day of the Lord will come as a thief in the night; in the which the heavens shall pass away with a great noise, and the elements shall melt with fervent heat, the earth also and the works that are therein shall be burned up (2 Peter 3:10).

A person believing in the Lord Jesus Christ needs to believe all the way through, because a very important truth about Christ is His return. As surely as you believe in His coming again it will affect you. Our Lord Jesus Christ, pointing out that nobody knew the day and the hour (not even the Son), told a parable of an evil servant who, because he thought that the master was not coming back any time soon, mistreated his fellow servants. The Lord told that parable by way of warning that no one knows when He is coming.

> And every man that hath this hope (the hope of seeing Jesus Christ in person) in him purifieth himself, even as he is pure (1 John 3:3).

This is one of the most dynamic of all truths. Some people feel that we would be motivated to do the will of God out of gratitude, inclined to serve God because He has done something for us, and inclined to turn to the Lord Jesus Christ because He died for us. All of which is true, but not the whole truth. The truth is that the Lord Jesus Christ is now alive. We should turn to Him not only because He once died for us but because He now lives for us. I can be grateful that Jesus Christ took my sins upon Himself and bore them away in His own body on the cross, and even now He intercedes on my behalf and prays for me every day. But more than that is true: He will come again. And those who will be with Him or will be here when He comes will see Him person to person.

In Second Peter 3:10 we have two aspects of the truth of the coming of the Lord: one refers to the time of His coming, and the other to the result of His coming. "But the day of the Lord will come as a thief in the night." This probably does not refer to any one calendar date; this is the time of His appearing. It might not be a twenty-four-hour period; it might be a split second, in the twinkling of an eye, at the last trumpet, that He will come. He will come in the clouds of heaven and in great glory.

This is not seen in the natural process; He is not coming as a result of anything going on in this world. There are things coming because of natural process: we have morning, noon, and night; we have the sun rising and setting. If the sun rises in the morning, it will set at night. We have springtime, summer, harvest, and winter. If you put your seed in the ground, later in the year will be the time of the harvest. This is predictable. But the coming of the Lord is not predictable in that fashion; it will not be the result of anything done in this world. It is in the will of God, part of an act of God. The day of the Lord will be according to the mind and will of God and as such it will come as a unit by itself like an act of God. When thieves come in the night, they are unexpected and unannounced. That is the way it will be with His coming, in such an hour as you think not.

There follows a description of what will happen, "The heavens shall pass away with a great noise, and the elements shall melt with fervent heat, the earth also and the works that are therein shall be burned up." Nobody really knows what fire is. What happens is according to the material: wood burns one way, cloth another; coal burns one way and straw burns another way, and oil burns differently. When we speak about the heavens burning, we do not know what the heavens are composed of, but when we speak about the earth burning, it will melt. Whatever the heavens are composed of, they will "pass away with a great noise, the elements shall melt with fervent heat, the earth also and the works that are therein shall be burned up." The description here is very much like the explosion of an atomic bomb.

PRESENT EFFECT OF THE WORLD'S END
(2 Peter 3:11-12)

Do you think it could have an effect on a person if he believed that the whole world might be destroyed suddenly?

> Seeing then that all these things shall be dissolved, what manner of persons ought ye to be in all holy conversation and godliness, looking for and hasting unto the coming of the day of God, wherein the heavens being on fire shall be dissolved, and the elements shall melt with fervent heat? (2 Peter 3:11-12).

What does the end of the world mean to people who believe it? Is this unsettling to people? It can be. Then shall we not believe it? Is it unsettling to think about dying? It depends entirely on what we base our thinking. The Bible warns us about expecting that we have a long time. The Lord Jesus told the story about a farmer who had such good crops his barns and granaries could not hold the produce.

> And he said, This will I do: I will pull down my barns, and build greater; and there will I bestow all my fruits and my goods. And I will say to my soul, Soul, thou hast much goods laid up for many years; take thine ease, eat, drink, and be merry. But God said unto him, Thou fool, this night thy soul shall be required of thee: then whose shall those things be, which thou hast provided? (Luke 12:18-20).

Scripture tells us that the coming of the Lord is something sure. Peter discussed what difference it will make. "Seeing then that all these things shall be dissolved, what manner of persons ought ye to be in all holy conversation and godliness." Some may think that "holy conversation" means being exceptionally spiritual, probably spending our time in praying or something of that nature. That would be a commendable practice but that is not what is meant by holy conversation. The word "holy" as an adjective means a hundred percent sincere, and conversation here means manner of life. So Peter asked what kind of person ought we to be in all our affairs. We should play it honest and straight. Godliness is that condition in you or in me when we are obedient to God and we respond to Him. It refers to an attitude of walking with the Lord and doing the things that are pleasing in His sight. "Looking for and hasting unto the coming of the day of God" means simply moving along day by day. A good phrase to use here would be anticipating it, expecting it, realizing there is nothing that will interfere with it. Here the phrase "the day of God" is used like "the day of the Lord" is used in verse 10: the time when God will reveal Himself, and the time when He will go into action, "wherein the heavens being on fire shall be dissolved."

Someone may say that if the heavens are to be dissolved, it must be going on now. How do we know it isn't going on now? You and I do not know. We do know that in the day of God the heavens will be on fire, and will be dissolved. The elements on earth shall melt with fervent heat. Inasmuch as it will happen that way, what kind of people ought we to be? We ought to be genuinely sincere and humbly walking with God.

THE EXPECTATION OF THE BELIEVER
(2 Peter 3:13-14)

Do you realize that the ultimate blessing every believer wants and longs for will be realized only after this world is destroyed?

> Nevertheless we, according to his promise, look for new heavens and a new earth, wherein dwelleth righteousness. Wherefore, beloved, seeing that ye look for such things, be diligent that ye may be found of him in peace, without spot, and blameless (2 Peter 3:13-14).

Inasmuch as this second epistle of Peter is written for believers in Christ, it would be more incredible if the coming of the Lord were talked about only with real believers. Those who accept the Bible as the Word of God and have accepted the Lord Jesus Christ personally do not have much trouble accepting what the Bible says about the end of the world. Peter wrote to believers in Christ not only about the end of the world, but to help them grow in spiritual matters. They will be stronger if they look forward to meeting Him face to face.

When Peter talked about the Lord Jesus Christ coming again he realized that he was confronting persons whom he called false teachers, persons who were presenting other ideas. For that reason Peter dwelt upon these things. He stated that no particular major event will occur between now and the end of time. In these verses he pointed to what is really assuring. He had been talking about calamities so far as this world is concerned, but believers in Christ are not limited to this world. This world will pass away; our bodies will pass away; everything that is material will pass away. However, we will not be suspended in space in a vacuum. A new situation will arise: a new heaven and a new earth.

Let me emphasize that the new will not emerge out of the old. It will replace the old. Something like this happens when a person becomes a believer in Christ. One does not become a believer in Christ because he was trained into it out of the past; it occurs when one is born again and something new is begun. It is something that happens in another way, like the breaking of day. It has been night time and now it changes to daylight. Night is first and the day follows, but it is important to notice that daylight does not come out of dark; daylight is daylight because of the sun. In other words, it is not by an evolutionary process. The new does not come out of the old as a product; it comes to replace the old.

So it is with reference to the things of God. With God and the Lord Jesus Christ at work there will be the new life. There will be a new heaven and a new earth, wherein dwelleth righteousness. This is just as it is with the born again person. It will be different. The new life in Christ Jesus is characterized by obedience, so the new heavens and the new earth are characterized by righteousness. The old heavens and the old earth have been marred by sin just as the old body is sinful; but by the grace of God we have heard the Gospel and have believed, and have been born again.

Peter continues, "Be diligent that ye may be found of him in peace." Whenever you see the words, "be diligent," this means the opposite of lazy. This very important truth could be neglected. Peter would not have been satisfied if what you believed had no effect on you. We have a part in spiritual living. We need to plant and to water, and God will give the increase. We need to read the Word of God and study, and God will bless our endeavors. "Be diligent that ye may be found of him in peace"—when you are being tested you will actually find that you are "in peace," that you have been blessed of God, having yielded to Him. "Without spot, and blameless." As surely as you confess your sin, He is faithful and just to forgive you your sin and to cleanse you from all unrighteousness. You can be without spot if you will just confess any known sin.

How can a believer be everything he is supposed to be? When Jesus of Nazareth was here the people asked what they should do that they might work the works of God. He replied, "This is the work of God, that ye believe on him whom he hath sent" (John 6:29). Put your whole trust in the Lord Jesus Christ and He will take care of you. Walk with Him and God will bless your soul.

SCRIPTURE MUST NOT BE TWISTED
(2 *Peter 3:15-16*)

Can you understand how some kinds of Bible study could be dangerous?

> And account that the long-suffering of our Lord is salvation; even as our beloved brother Paul also according to the wisdom given unto him hath written unto you; as also in all his epistles, speaking in them of these things; in which are some things hard to be understood, which they that are unlearned and unstable wrest, as they do also the other scriptures, unto their own destruction (2 Peter 3:15-16).

In the actual work of salvation let us start with Calvary. Christ Jesus died for us and He was raised from the dead as our

Savior. The death and resurrection of the Lord Jesus Christ can be presented to any human being, so that he can be invited to accept Jesus Christ as his Savior. Christ Jesus is our substitutionary sacrifice, having died for us; and we put our trust in Him. For many people this is as far as the thinking goes. But this is the start of spiritual experience. Jesus lived in the presence of His disciples for some forty days after His resurrection. Then came His ascension into heaven in full view of all. After that He sent forth His Holy Spirit into their hearts. The Holy Spirit shows us even now what our living Lord Jesus Christ wants to do through us.

In addition, the Lord Jesus Christ did something after Pentecost which He is still doing right now. He is at the right hand of God the Father, making intercession for the believer. It is this truth that is essential if the believer is to enter into communion with Christ. There is yet one more thing true about the Lord Jesus Christ. He will come again in what the Bible speaks of as the "Parousia." He will appear in this world. The coming again of the Lord Jesus Christ will be a strong testimony to the world and a witness in service.

Second Peter 3:15-16 gives a very simple statement that we are to "account that the long-suffering of our Lord is salvation." Where we see that word "long-suffering" we should look at the same word in verse 9: God is not now revealing the day of judgment; He is not now bringing people into His presence to judge their eternal destiny. He is waiting so that others might come to know the Lord Jesus Christ because God is not willing that any should perish but that all should have everlasting life.

"Even as our beloved brother Paul also according to the wisdom given unto him hath written unto you." It is interesting to read here how Peter refers to Paul, since in the Book of Galatians we read that Paul withstood Peter when Peter was not following the truth in the light of the Gospel. Peter evidently held no rancor. How they conducted themselves is a tribute to both.

"In which are some things hard to be understood (many people who read Paul would agree with that), which they that are unlearned and unstable wrest." This word "wrest" is a root of the word "wrestle." Have you ever seen two men wrestle? They twist each other, each trying to force the other out of place. There are persons who do that with the Scriptures. They will take a certain passage and twist it around, forcing that Scripture out of its context; as they "do also the other scriptures, unto their own destruction." That is why some Bible study can be dangerous. Anyone who tries to fit the Scriptures into an idea of his own is in danger. A person can go wrong with his own interpretation of any passage of Scripture.

The word "unlearned" in this passage does not mean they have not been to the university; they are "unlearned" with reference to the Scriptures. "Unstable" means they are not totally committed to the Lord Jesus Christ. If a person interprets Scripture with the idea he believes the Bible, then later he says he does not know for sure; that kind of back and forth—now you are in, now you are out—frame of mind, is what is meant by "unstable." James tells us that "a double-minded man" going in two directions is "unstable in all his ways. Let not that man think that he shall receive any thing of the Lord." Those who twist the Scriptures in this fashion will suffer the result of their own mishandling of Scripture. They will be led into their own destruction.

AN EARNEST WARNING
(2 Peter 3:17-18)

Do you realize that you cannot stand still being a Christian? Either you will serve the Lord more or you will begin to doubt.

> Ye therefore, beloved, seeing ye know these things before, beware lest ye also, being led away with the error of the wicked, fall from your own steadfastness. But grow in grace, and in the knowledge of our Lord and Saviour Jesus Christ. To him be glory both now and for ever. Amen (2 Peter 3:17-18).

A real problem for all believers in Christ is, among other things, that of false teachers who claim to teach the truth. Their technique is notorious: they speak flattery to people; they make the hearer feel that he can do everything, if he just starts right. Then they promise to help him get started right. In general these false teachers are alike in one respect: they move attention away from the living Lord, and tend to focus attention upon themselves or upon other human beings. This gives them a sense of real assurance.

Peter bluntly exposes these false teachers as being dangerous to the welfare of God's people. To meet the problem of the spiritual need of God's people, Peter discusses the return of Christ. He made it a point to tell people what the wrong leaders were saying and doing. A believer can be led away through the error of the wicked. The error of the wicked will not look wicked. If it did, you would not succumb. The word "wicked" does not mean "immoral"; if it meant immoral some believers would not have any trouble. Believers in Christ will not be immoral. Neither does "wicked" mean uncouth or vulgar; if it meant that some believers would not be interested. And it does not mean vicious; most believers in Christ would never be vicious. In the original language the Hebrew word "wicked" means that you can be wicked in traveling on the highway. It means that you are on the wrong road. For those who know anything about flying airplanes, it means that you are "off the beam," you have missed your "landing strip."

The Bible says: "Let the wicked forsake his ways." Let the man who is headed in the wrong direction return to the Lord; He will have mercy on him. Now there are other words for evil and for sin, but this word for wicked simply means "off the way." When you let anything divert you from thinking about the Lord Jesus Christ, your attention is easily captured and directed to your personal interest. Peter would say you would be walking after your own lust, your own desire. Are you acquainted with what happens when a person tries to cross a strange section of country covered with trees, going through a forest? The common danger for a newcomer is to think he is walking due east or due north, but if he walks long enough he will come back to where he was. He will walk in a circle. This is not peculiar; it is natural. Men have tried to figure out why they walk in a circle, and they have decided it is because of inner tensions. The only way to get out of the forest is to line up trees, and keep them lined up in front of you. Walk in a straight line and you will get out of the woods. Men who fly at night know this is true. They undergo careful training and discipline because, if they follow their own feelings, their own inward consciousness, they would think they were going straight, when actually they were going to the left.

I am talking about "walking after their own desires," following their own inner tensions. There is only one sure deliverance: walk in the Lord. Go straight. There is one solution to the whole problem; go God's way and you will not go wrong. Believe in the Lord Jesus Christ and you will not believe error. Read and study the Bible and you will know what is right. Keep the truth of the Lord Jesus Christ: His virgin birth, His life, His miracle working power, His death, His resurrection, and His future coming again.

Put your trust in Him. He will be your Savior. This was the message of Peter in his second epistle.

JUDE

† † †

THIS LETTER IS A WARNING
(Jude 1-4)

Can you see why believers have the need to supervise what is being taught among them?

The book of Jude is the last epistle in the New Testament canon before the Book of Revelation. It is a short book consisting of one chapter with 25 verses. Apparently it is quite unknown. But though small, this book is by no means light or insignificant. If it were the only Scripture dealing with the peril of false teaching one could understand the common aversion to the message which is almost exactly like that contained in Second Peter. Paul, in Second Timothy, speaks about these matters also.

As he begins his letter, Jude admits he had not intended to devote his letter to this problem. He had intended to write about their common salvation; to talk about the spiritual experience of trusting in the Lord. But he chose to discuss the problem of being faithful to the revealed Word because he felt that it was necessary.

The general attitude among believers toward others has generally been tolerant and flexible. Believers are so interested in winning souls they will put up with almost anything if they can just get a hearing from the people they are seeking to reach. And they are so humble in rating themselves they are willing to make adjustments to anybody. Even when others differ, believers are inclined to think they should accommodate themselves graciously to those who differ. They have their own convictions, but they feel almost as though they should let other people have theirs. They hesitate to judge others, and they especially feel hesitant to condemn anybody. But the Book of Jude emphasizes the responsibility by all who know the truth to do this very thing.

There can be situations among believers that make it necessary to "call out the troops," when they will have to "man the ramparts." In reading this short epistle one can appreciate Jude as a man of few words, who speaks directly to the point. "Jude, the servant of Jesus Christ, and brother of James" (Jude 1); with reference to self, that is all he has to say. He is the servant of Jesus Christ. This sounds like Paul, the "bondslave." It was the general attitude of the apostles, the one thing that marked them. It was as though Jude, standing in a large company, might be asked, "And who are you?" His reply would be simple, "The servant of Jesus Christ." We know nothing else about him. We do not know his trade nor how he occupied himself. That was not important at this point. Jude was going to talk about the Gospel. He was going to say something about spiritual life, and he wanted it understood that what he said and what he did were being said and done as by the servant of Jesus Christ.

"And brother of James." There are a number of men in the New Testament who are called James. Scholars have tried to distinguish them, but the result is not clear. Jude identified himself only as being the brother of a certain man whom they knew.

> Jude, the servant of Jesus Christ, and brother of James, to them that are sanctified by God the Father, and preserved in Jesus Christ, and called (Jude 1).

These three things are what he had to say about the believers: "sanctified by God the Father" (and from other translations I gather this brings out the idea of being dearly loved, or beloved, set apart by the love of God); "and preserved in Jesus Christ" (an interesting word about salvation, "kept safe"); "and called" (a New Testament reference to believers). Basically "called" simply means "chosen." It is also translated as the word "elect," which does not mean "select." Jude had been called of God through the Gospel and he had responded. These are the things that count about any believer.

Mercy unto you, and peace, and love, be multiplied (Jude 2).

This seems the standard greeting of an apostle. It is a prayer. This is what Jude wanted God to bestow upon "them that are sanctified by God the Father, and preserved in Jesus Christ, and called." In these simple words profound truth is implied: believers need the mercy of God that they might have peace and be blessed with the love of God.

> Beloved, when I gave all diligence to write unto you of the common salvation, it was needful for me to write unto you, and exhort you that ye should earnestly contend for the faith which was once delivered unto the saints (Jude 3).

Jude appealed to them to contend for the faith which was once for all handed down to the saints. He was referring to the sum of Christian belief which had been delivered verbally to the holy people of God.

Jude's thought is expressed in another translation: "I had been planning to write you some thoughts about the salvation God has given us, but now I find I must write of something else instead, urging you to stoutly defend the truth which God gave, once for all, to His people to keep without change through the years."

Another translator uses words like this, "Being very eager to write to you of our common salvation, I found it necessary to write appealing to you to contend for the faith which was once for all delivered to the saints." Jude implied it was most important, not so much to understand more deeply what believers had in the Gospel, but to make sure that they kept what they had.

The need for Jude to do this was stated thus:

> For there are certain men crept in unawares, who were before of old ordained to this condemnation, ungodly men, turning the grace of our God into lasciviousness, and denying the only Lord God, and our Lord Jesus Christ (Jude 4).

Another translation puts it this way: "For certain men have crept in stealthily, gaining entrance secretly by a side door." Such persons were teaching in the group of believers and we need to be aware that it can be true among us today. Here is yet another translation, "I say this because some godless teachers have wormed their way in among you, saying that after we become Christians we can do just as we like without fear of God's punishment. The fate of such people was written long ago, for they have turned against our only Master and Lord, Jesus Christ."

That was the beginning of the warning given in this letter. As a minister of the Gospel, I have a responsibility, all of us have a responsibility, to make sure that the Gospel, which has been revealed from God in the person of the Lord Jesus Christ as recorded in the Scriptures, shall be told as it is without compromise or change so that people might know the truth: that they might be saved.

THE JUDGMENT OF GOD IS SURE
(Jude 5-9)

Does it seem strange that an apostle of Jesus Christ should gravely warn his readers that God will destroy the ungodly?

So much has been said about the grace of God, and about the humility and meekness of Christ Jesus, it is to be feared that many may think that God will not destroy. I have heard people say earnestly that God will not destroy anything that He made. But with Scriptures in hand, we have to say we know He will. Sometimes persons have the idea that while judgment and destruction, such as the story of the flood and of Israel invading Canaan and destroying the Canaanites are in the Old Testament, such ideas are out of place in the New Testament. But there is a corrective for that.

Jesus warned cities about the judgment of God.

> Then began he to upbraid the cities wherein most of his mighty works were done, because they repented not: Woe unto thee, Chorazin! woe unto thee, Bethsaida! for if the mighty works, which were done in you, had been done in Tyre and Sidon, they would have repented long ago in sackcloth and ashes. But I say unto you, It shall be more tolerable for Tyre and Sidon at the day of judgment, than for you. And thou, Capernaum, which are exalted unto heaven, shalt be brought down to hell: for if the mighty works, which have been done in thee, had been done in Sodom, it would have remained until this day (Matt. 11:20-23).

Such were the words of Jesus. He also warned people who were doing injustice to children and misleading those who were dependent upon them:

> But whoso shall offend one of these little ones which believe in me, it were better for him that a millstone were hanged about his neck, and that he were drowned in the depth of the sea (Matt. 18:6).

In his epistles Paul described the wrath of God as it came upon some. For instance, in the first chapter of Romans we read God gave certain persons over to unclean affections, to a reprobate mind (Romans 1:24-28). Paul knew he was preaching the truth and warned:

> If any man preach any other gospel unto you than that ye have received, let him be accursed (Gal. 1:9).

The book of Hebrews shows that the New Testament has this same message of warning concerning those who have in any way disobeyed and become ungodly.

> For if we sin willfully after that we have received the knowledge of the truth, there remaineth no more sacrifice for sins, but a certain fearful looking for of judgment and fiery indignation, which shall devour the adversaries. He that despised Moses' law died without mercy under two or three witnesses: of how much sorer punishment, suppose ye, shall he be thought worthy, who hath trodden under foot the Son of God, and hath counted the blood of the covenant, wherewith he was sanctified, an unholy thing, and hath done despite unto the Spirit of grace? For we know him that hath said, Vengeance belongeth unto me, I will recompense, saith the Lord. And again, The Lord shall judge his people. It is a fearful thing to fall into the hands of the living God (Heb. 10:26-31).

Peter is even more outspoken in the second chapter of his second book (2 Peter 2:1-22). Here in this book of Jude the Holy Spirit brings the truth forward plainly:

> I will therefore put you in remembrance, though ye once knew this, how that the Lord, having saved the people out of the land of Egypt, afterward destroyed them that believed not (Jude 5).

Someone may say that if He brought them out He would certainly not destroy them. But here is another translation, "Now I want to remind you, though you were fully informed once for all, that though the Lord at one time delivered a people out of the land of Egypt, He subsequently destroyed those of them who did not believe—who refused to adhere to, trust in and rely upon Him."

> And the angels which kept not their first estate, but left their own habitation, he hath reserved in everlasting chains under darkness unto the judgment of the great day (Jude 6).

First, Jude went into Old Testament history about the children of Israel. Here he writes about what happened in the spiritual world with the fallen angels. Another writer expressed this passage this way: "And angels that did not keep (care for, guard and hold to) their own first place of power but abandoned their proper dwelling place, He has reserved in custody in eternal chains (bonds) under the thick gloom of utter darkness until the judgment and doom of the great day."

Jude is warning his people that nobody can play fast and loose with God. Another writer translating this same verse about the angels says, "And I remind you of those angels who were once pure and holy, but willingly turned to a life of sin. Now God has them chained up in prisons of darkness, waiting for the judgment day."

> Even as Sodom and Gomorrah, and the cities about them in like manner, giving themselves over to fornication, and going after strange flesh, are set forth for an example, suffering the vengance of eternal fire (Jude 7).

Another translation reads, "Just as Sodom and Gomorrah and the adjacent towns, which likewise gave themselves over to impurity and indulged in unnatural vice and sensual perversity, are laid out (in plain sight) as an exhibit of perpetual punishment (to warn) of everlasting fire (the wicked are sentenced to suffer)." It is apparent that the Holy Spirit led Jude to add another instance of the judgment of God.

This Scripture passage gives repeated illustrations of God bringing judgment. He will bring judgment where some might think He would spare. For example, Jude wrote of people delivered from Egypt, who later, because they were not wholly yielded to God, were destroyed. This happened not to all but to certain ones. These things are written for an example to us that judgment should not come upon us the way it came upon them (1 Cor. 10:6, 11). Then again Jude referred to the fallen angels. One would not think ordinarily of angels falling from their high estate, but some did: and these are being kept now to be destroyed.

Following this Jude used another illustration, "These cities of the plain." Wickedness was probably everywhere, but some places were more wicked than others. The disaster that came upon Sodom and Gomorrah was a demonstration of the judgment of God. It was an area-wide catastrophe that destroyed Sodom and Gomorrah, and other villages and towns. All were alike in that they had given themselves over to fornication and going after strange flesh. They were notoriously immoral, and God brought judgment upon them. Jude then made a direct application:

> Likewise also these filthy dreamers defile the flesh, despise dominion, and speak evil of dignities (Jude 8).

By way of emphasizing their wickedness Jude made a comparison,

> Yet Michael the archangel, when contending with the devil he disputed about the body of Moses, durst not bring against him a railing accusation, but said, The Lord rebuke thee (Jude 9).

THE UNGODLY ARE DOOMED
(Jude 9-16)

Do you realize that a person can be ungodly without being vulgar or obscene or profane?

Two of the basic evils in the world today are disrespect for those who are in authority, and widespread deception among men. Things are not what they seem and men are aften not what they claim to be. At no time is anything more dangerous than when poison is mingled with food, or when dishonest men associate with men of virtue. When they are all together it is difficult to know which is which. We are particularly concerned about those who say they are believers in Christ when they really are not. As I think about what needs to be said, I must humbly admit I am glad it is written in the Bible.

In this book of Jude, judgment is expressed upon evil men

among the believers in a way that is frightening. Jude points out to believers that among them are men who are dangerous, because they are untrue. Because the relationship with Christ is spiritual, it is invisible. One cannot tell by looking at a man whether or not he really believes in the Lord and whether he is committed to the Lord. Of course, we look for certain actions that we expect and we look for certain conduct we think would naturally follow, but actions and conduct can be imitated. Because this is so, deception is easy and can be made to appear natural.

The Scriptures say that by their fruit you shall know them. Jude described the consequences of ungodliness. This conduct can be found among us today. Jude refers to an Old Testament event to emphasize this matter of disrespect.

> Yet Michael the archangel, when contending with the devil he disputed about the body of Moses, durst not bring against him a railing accusation, but said, The Lord rebuke thee (Jude 9).

When the mighty angel Michael confronted Satan about the body of Moses he dared not bring against Satan a railing accusation, as if he were despising him. Satan is evil, but Satan is powerful. And Michael, confronting him, does not presume to show disrespect to this mighty creature. He humbly calls upon God to rebuke him: "The Lord rebuke thee."

Jude had said earlier, "These filthy dreamers defile the flesh, despise dominion, and speak evil of dignities." Now he continued to speak about these people.

> But these speak evil of those things which they know not . . .(Jude 10).

It is disturbing to hear the loose speech of people who do not know what they are talking about, casting aspersion on the things of the Gospel. Jude says plainly, "But what they know naturally, as brute beasts, in those things they corrupt themselves" (Jude 10).

When reading this in our English language we could feel that Jude despised them; but when Jude speaks of these "brute beasts" he simply means animals, not human beings. If you look around, you will find most people acting naturally, just as animals do. There are many things about the conduct of a human being that parallels the conduct of animals, brute beasts that go by their senses; that is the meaning here. In those things they corrupt themselves, and so it is with human beings.

Jude then refers to three instances of rebellion against God; three people who knew something about Him.

> Woe unto them! for they have gone in the way of Cain, and ran
> greedily after the error of Balaam for reward, and perished in
> the gainsaying of Korah (Jude 11).

You remember Cain succumbed to jealousy and envy. Cain knew God well enough to deal with Him, but he would not honor Him. He was jealous of his brother and eventually committed murder.

"And ran greedily after the error of Balaam for reward." Balaam was that prophet who advised against Israel, and he did it for money. He was bought and paid for, the classic example in the Bible of a priest who used his function to make money. And these people ran greedily after the error Balaam made. He knew the truth but he cooperated with those people who were against him.

"And perished in the gainsaying of Korah." In the case of Korah there was rebellion against authority. He complained that Moses and Aaron took too much on themselves. So Jude used these three instances to describe three ungodly persons who knew something about God but who disobeyed Him.

And now in verses 12 and 13, in further describing these deceitful persons, Jude used a number of figures of speech. "These are spots in your feasts of charity." The meaning in the original language is more like "hidden stones in the river," like a hidden sandbar or a reef upon which one could wreck. In other words, the only way the word "spot" could be used would be to say "danger spot." "When they feast with you, feeding themselves without fear." These people were stuffing themselves without regard to others. They would be present at congregational fellowships and take full advantage of all the goodwill that prevailed among the believing people, even though personally they did not believe. "Clouds they are without water, carried about of winds." Naturally a cloud is expected to bring rain. In a time of drought we look up into the sky and see a cloud forming, and we hope it will bring rain. But the wind blows it away. Such clouds make a big show with no results. "Trees whose fruit withereth, without fruit, twice dead, plucked up by the roots." When you come to a fruit tree you expect fruit but these do not have any. "Raging waves of the sea, foaming out their own shame."

There is more in Jude's description of these persons. "Wandering stars, to whom is reserved the blackness of darkness for ever." These are hard statements.

> And Enoch also, the seventh from Adam, prophesied of these, saying, Behold, the Lord cometh with ten thousands of his saints, to execute judgment upon all, and to convince all that are ungodly among them of all their ungodly deeds which they have ungodly committed, and of all their hard speeches which ungodly sinners have spoken against him. These are murmurers, complainers, walking after their own lusts; and their mouth speaketh great swelling words, having men's persons in admiration because of advantage (Jude 14-16).

Thus Jude described dangerous "spots" among believers. What a revelation of our danger every day! We cannot always trust people, even among believers who profess faith. Trust in God. Many times these people cannot know what they are doing. We can pray for them, but we should not trust them. "Cursed be the man that trusteth in man, and maketh flesh his arm, and whose heart departeth from the Lord" (Jer. 17:5).

BELIEVERS MUST STAND STEADFAST
(Jude 17-21)

Can you see where there would be danger when the Gospel is ridiculed?

It is easy to forget that ridicule and sarcasm actually can be harmful. Have you ever wondered why so few people are willing to be openly associated with the name of Jesus Christ? Many feel a hesitancy about mentioning the name of Jesus Christ in public. In recent years it has become somewhat easier to speak of "Jesus," but I notice a strange aversion to His title, "Christ." Many talk about worshiping and walking with Jesus in such a way that one wonders if they really know what they are talking about. When they do not give Him His title, Christ Jesus, one can be sure something is missing. When students are asked to rate the great men of history, Jesus of Nazareth is often overlooked. The Gospel of the Lord Jesus Christ is a well known message and the whole work of the Lord Jesus Christ is well known. We all know there was such a person who lived and died; the cross of Calvary stands on the horizon of history in plain relief. Something of the importance of the Lord Jesus Christ is implied in the fact that we date time from His birth, yet oftentimes what happened to the Lord Jesus Christ is ignored.

Shouldn't we be concerned about this? Do you think it makes any difference to your children and to young people that they are growing up in a culture where a large part of the truth is ignored? Does it matter that Christ died for us? Then why don't we think about it and talk about it? It is dangerous to ignore it, and apparently Jude thought so.

> But, beloved, remember ye the words which were spoken before of the apostles of our Lord Jesus Christ; how that they told you there should be mockers in the last time, who should walk after their own ungodly lusts. These be they who separate themselves, sensual, having not the Spirit (Jude 17-19).

This reminds us of the words of the Apostle Paul to the elders at Ephesus.

> For I know this, that after my departing shall grievous wolves enter in among you, not sparing the flock (Acts 20:29).

And when he wrote to Timothy, Paul said,

> Now the Spirit speaketh expressly, that in the latter times some shall depart from the faith, giving heed to seducing spirits, and doctrines of devils (1 Tim. 4:1).

And again,

> This know also, that in the last days perilous times shall come (2 Tim. 3:1).

In that same passage he says,

> But evil men and seducers shall wax worse and worse, deceiving, and being deceived (2 Tim. 3:13).

Paul wrote to Titus,

> For there are many unruly and vain talkers and deceivers, . . .
> whose mouths must be stopped (Titus 1:10-11).

In the second chapter of Second Peter this condition is dwelt upon at length, and one may wonder why God allows these deceivers to continue to contaminate others as they do. One may also ask why God allows Satan. We do not know. What we *do* know is that Satan has his messengers working.

Jude wrote:

> How that they told you there should be mockers in the last time, who should walk after their own ungodly lusts (Jude 18).

Again, Peter wrote:

> Knowing this first, that there shall come in the last days scoffers, walking after their own lusts (2 Peter 3:3).

Jude continued in verse 19, "These be they who separate themselves, sensual, having not the Spirit." The word "sensual" is to be understood as the word natural, going by their senses. Agitators will cause divisions, and worldly-minded people will associate with the believers.

> But ye, beloved, building up yourselves on your most holy faith, praying in the Holy Ghost, keep yourselves in the love of God, looking for the mercy of our Lord Jesus Christ unto eternal life (Jude 20-21).

My dear fellow-believers, we must build up our lives ever more strongly upon the foundation of our faith, learning to pray in the power and strength of the Holy Spirit. Whatever can we do? The word is "believe." And for believing, study the Bible, join Bible classes, and go to a church where the minister believes and preaches the Bible. This is most important. "Keep yourselves in the love of God, looking for the mercy of our Lord Jesus Christ unto eternal life." We should stay always within the boundaries where God can reach us and bless us. We must wait patiently for the eternal life that our Lord Jesus Christ in His mercy is going to give us.

In a time of conflict, confusion, and chaos we should go to the sanctuaries and into the presence of God. Today we are being affected by considerable controversy in some of our churches, and some people are protesting against looseness and waywardness, while others protest against the protester. I would say to you, let us look up into the face of the Lord Jesus Christ and have this in mind: our souls are at stake, everything is at stake. We need the help of God and He will provide for us. Let us put our trust in Him.

THE BELIEVER IS SAFE IN THE LORD
(Jude 22-25)

In a day of turmoil and danger, how can a believer be confident?

> Now unto him that is able to keep you from falling, and to present you faultless before the presence of his glory with exceeding joy, to the only wise God our Saviour, be glory and majesty, dominion and power, both now and ever. Amen (Jude 24-25).

These are the words with which Jude concludes his message. This epistle is the most pointed against heresy in the Scriptures. You will remember when Jude began his letter his original intention had been to discuss the common salvation, but he felt he should warn them of dangers caused by false teachers among them. Jude contains the strongest message about false teachers, and the impression is deep and clear. Danger for believers is to be found within the company of those who profess to believe in the Lord Jesus Christ.

It is a true fact, and let us just admit it carefully and sadly: some are going to hell. Some who profess to believe are going to hell, and they seek to seduce others to go with them. I do not believe they realize they are going to hell. They do not think anything bad is going to happen. They probably think they are on a rosy path to a blessed fellowship or a wonderful experience of some kind, and they want others to come along. They find people who believe the Bible, so they attempt to show how the Bible is not true. They see people who are committed to the Lord Jesus Christ, and they claim the Gospel is just an old story or a myth. They seek to destroy confidence in the Scriptures. Then they paint a wonderful picture of what is going to happen to them, and others are invited to come along.

Regardless of what manner their course takes, I am satisfied they do not realize what their end will be. But Jude knew. He warned the believers that these persons dwelt among them and would seek to ensnare them. Jude warns that the danger is real. Believers must be alert. It is not enough to know that Christ Jesus came for me. That is wonderful. But it is not enough to know that God will receive me in Christ. That is also wonderful, as is the fact that God has given me the Holy Spirit to guide me. But I have the responsibility to strengthen and feed my faith.

A person is not born with faith in God, although we are born with the capacity to believe. Faith cometh by hearing and hearing by the Word of God. Because of this believers should be diligent in reading the Scriptures and diligent in cultivating prayer. They should be diligent in fellowship with believers, in attending the public worship of God, and in joining with others in the service of God. Believers need to exercise diligence about all these matters.

Jude pointed out that not everyone on the wrong road is malicious, or is even to be blamed. Some who are on the wrong road do not know better; no one ever told them. This may be the reason why Jude used words like this:

> And of some have compassion, making a difference: and others save with fear, pulling them out of the fire; hating even the garment spotted by the flesh (Jude 22-23).

Although we need not associate with these people who are wrong, at the same time we do not hate them. We mean them no harm. Wherever there is one among them who is actually innocent in his foolishness (if that can be possible) and does not realize how far wrong he is, Jude said "Of some have compassion"; or, as another translator expresses it, "And convict some who dispute with you, and on some have mercy who waver and doubt." Try to help those who argue against you. Be merciful and convince some, especially those who doubt. "And others save with fear, pulling them out of the fire; hating even the garment spotted by the flesh."

Apparently there are people who can be saved from this fate. He says to strive to save others, snatching them out of the fire. "On others take pity with fear, loathing even the garment spotted by the flesh and polluted by their sensuality." Another translator puts it this way: "Save some by snatching them as from the very flames of hell itself. And as for others, help them to find the Lord by being kind to them, but be careful that you yourselves aren't pulled along into their sins. Hate every trace of their sin while being merciful to them as sinners." This is the word Jude would press upon believing people.

As we think of such different people and attitudes this question comes to mind: How can we be sure of anything? Then Jude gives expression to one of the greatest Scriptures written,

> Now unto him that is able to keep you from falling, and to present you faultless before the presence of his glory with exceeding joy, to the only wise God our Saviour, be glory and majesty, dominion and power, both now and ever. Amen (Jude 24-25).

Here is something very important for us; because of the dangers, snares, and stumbling blocks that we encounter in our living as believers, Jude directs attention to the source of security: the only wise God, our Savior. Man does not have the strength to avoid falling, nor the wisdom to avoid stumbling. He must have help; he must have someone to hold him up. But that help will never be in himself. It will be *for* him, never *in* him. God is able to keep us from falling and He can do more than that. God is able and ready to present the believer faultless before the presence of His glory with exceeding joy. Just think of it! Not only is it true that God can keep me, but that God can bring me to Himself! Not only that He will sustain me so that I do not fall, but He will bring me to Himself.

The believer need not have fear about his future. The work of Christ is not only retroactive, in that He died for my past sins and delivers me from judgment; but the work of Christ is also an anticipation. He not only died to save me from the sins I have committed, He died and was raised again to save me from the sins I could have committed, that I would have committed, if it had not been for Him. The wonderful truth of the Gospel is that God intends to bring the believer into glory, to the praise of His holy name.